Considerations in Making Money

Book 1 Beyond Success Series

by

Mary Čolak

Published in 2022 by Discourse Books, Victoria, BC, Canada

www.marycolak.com

Cover design by impact studios

Library and Archives Canada Cataloguing in Publication

Considerations in making money:
Book 1 beyond success series / Mary Čolak

Includes bibliographical footnotes.

Paperback: ISBN 978-1-7778086-0-0

Electronic book: ISBN 978-1-7778086-2-4

1. Business & Economics / Finance / Wealth Management
2. Business & Economics / Personal Success
3. Self-help / Personal Growth / Success

Dedication

I dedicate this book with love to my family.

****

To all those who ever wanted lots of money:
I wish for you an income that disgusts people.

How is it possible that money cannot buy
happiness?
I assure you, money can and does buy happiness.

Acknowledgments

Thank you to all those that made this book possible: my bank, my husband—*Nikola* (aka "Nick") (who is usually my bank), my book cover designer—*impact studios*, my book publisher—*Discourse Books*, my book distributor—*Lachesis Publishing*, and all those that encouraged me to "just do it."

I drew wisdom from all those I met through the years—my friends, colleagues, clients, and mentors—you may not know it, but all our interactions, especially your advice and encouragement, stuck with me. I am grateful for our encounters.

Reviews

"High praise for Mary's first book. Her writing is clear, direct, and informative, with just the right touch of playfulness to make even the hardened reader smile. You'll find topics here that you may not have ever considered concerning money."

—*Dr. Marina Uzelac, Chiropractor, Wholistic Chiropractic & Wellness*

"Mary is a gifted writer. Her mastery shows even in her first book. I was impressed at how she skillfully pieced together seemingly unrelated topics into a cohesive gem that makes one think about different aspects of money. Is money one of the most important things in life?
This book will enlighten you to think of all possibilities, whether business or personal profit is your goal."

—*Lori Roter, MA CRM PMP*

"Money is always a foundational piece in life. Mary covers all the bases to help businesses and others carefully consider where they spend their money. This book is a great read—straightforward and value-packed."

—*Dr. Michael Dujela, Surgeon, Washington Orthopaedic Center*

Coming Soon

Beyond Success Series Books

Acquiring Time

Lean Productivity and Efficiency

Communicating for Results

Getting a Handle on Records

Considerations for Making Money
Book 1 Beyond Success Series

Contents

Introduction

Do you have enough money? I wish I could say that I did, although I certainly don't—but some days I suppose that I do, although I imagine the bigger question is how much money is enough? And who or what precisely quantifies "enough money?"

If you are the quantifier, how do you know when you have enough? Is it because you own one car or a garage full of antique cars? Or is it because you can afford to take public transportation everywhere? Or do you even need material possessions to quantify having enough money? I imagine we do need material things. Otherwise, what is the point of money?

A banker friend told me that a mindset of "saving is good" is bad. Having enough money is not about how much you make or save. It's about how much you invest. Consider this: if you save money, then inflation works against your saved stash of cash, eating away at the value of your money every minute that you do nothing with it. That is why it's a good idea to invest your money— stockpiled cash does no good for anyone. For example, consider investing in such things as real estate, gold, bonds, or other commodities.

Another key to profits is diversifying your investments. In other words, don't put all your eggs in one basket. However, the question then becomes how much money should you place in each basket? Unfortunately, I cannot help guide you in that aspect—your financial planner or banker are great go-to people. Still, I can help you understand how you can profit in different business or personal areas.

There is no doubt that money is an exciting topic. It can be a hot question in boardrooms and bedrooms, but not the kind of "hot" you're thinking about when it's in the bedroom.

Many people will tell you that money isn't everything. For example, they say that love, relationships, and family all trump money. But I don't buy it (no pun intended). And if love is all you need, then where does money fit? Those who have ever been in love claim that love is incredible in the early days. Of course, that's true because the body is swooning in oxytocin, the love hormone. But a year into the relationship, if you are moving from job to job to make ends meet, your lack of stable employment may eclipse love. Likewise, living on debt can suck you dry—I've been there, done that.

And relationships? It's the same thing. We can rely on our friends to bail us out of jams but only for so long—eventually, our friends grow tired of always giving but never getting anything in return. The same goes for family—dependable family steps in to help—until they don't. Then, if we never have enough money to give ourselves the things we truly deserve and enjoy, the family gets to a point where they cannot keep enabling the same "going nowhere" behaviours. Fair point. Yes, money is an interesting phenomenon. You cannot live without it, no matter who says that you can. But is it the key to everything?

From a business and personal perspective, I believe that money is power. People have made this a fact. But, can people be powerful if they don't have money? Yes, some can be, for example, Martin Luther King, Mahatma Gandhi, Mother Teresa, Charles Darwin, Rosa Parks, and Nikola Tesla; however, we cannot discount money as a critical influence ingredient.

I hope this short collection of my favorite posts about money and related topics gives you a new perspective on money and prosperity. Perhaps it will encourage you to work harder and make more money. Or maybe it will do the opposite. Either way, I wish you a world of success that includes the means and ability to have enough money to purchase all the material things you desire, whether it is through your business operations or regular "9-to-5" gigs.

When you have enough money, you will find that life is less stressful in all areas.

The Skinny on How Money Got Here

Money has a fascinating past. Did you know that the first form of money was the Mesopotamian shekel? It arose around 5,000 years ago. Before then, people were perfectly happy bartering. For instance, there were rich dowries to attract a husband, alcohol and fresh livestock to pay for medical visits, land title transfers to quash jail terms—you know, the stuff that still probably occurs today in some regions of our world.

Taxation also came into existence around 3,000 B.C. in Egypt. Numerous historical documents mention this fact, including the Bible. In the early days, exchanges and trades worked quite well in small communities where people could remember who owed whom. However, as the community grew, keeping tabs became a bit more complicated. This difficulty forced people to start trading objects as a type of IOU.[1] People exchanged items like whales' teeth for safekeeping until they paid their debt—this type of safekeeping

---

[1] An IOU is a phonetic acronym of the words "I owe you." This document is often viewed as an informal written agreement rather than a legally binding commitment. The IOU dates as far back as the 18th century, at least. Today, IOUs are still very much in use.

reminds me of today's pawnbrokers.[2] What is even more interesting before the invention of money is that people invented debt with these IOUs.

When people started using money, they noticed one crucial thing: money made you powerful. Not only that, if you were powerful, it meant you could get more money. Read that again.

Eventually, people introduced metal money after trying various other forms like barley and shells. But they soon found that metal was too heavy to carry around (much like tons of barley and sea shells), so they invented paper money. We credit the Chinese with the paper money invention. They started keeping their metal money in their palaces while issuing IOUs for long-distance trading. Metal is heavy to lug around. With increasing global trade, concern grew over how easy it is to print paper money, so the Chinese linked the value of money to gold, but today, we still rely on goods and money exchanges. Valuing money against a gold standard went by the wayside in the 1970s.

Through the years, starting in the 16th century, when Spain brought home massive additional supplies of precious metals, inflation

---

2 A pawnbroker is a person who lends money at interest in exchange for an article that they keep as security until your debt is paid.

became a thing. With their newfound purchasing power using more money (the precious metals), merchants increased their prices. Therefore, the returning explorers were no further ahead, and if they did not have the new gold (i.e., the precious metals), they were worse off. Thus, added supplies and discrepancies in purchasing power led to inflation.

Inflation is an interesting manmade phenomenon. Too much money chasing too few goods causes inflation. Therefore, producers produced more goods or slowed down the circulation of the new money supply to counteract inflation. Slowing down the money supply means people saved more, spent less.

In the 18th century, the British made it illegal for their colonies to print money. Instead, they forced the colonies to trade with the motherland. According to Benjamin Franklin,[3] the burden of British taxation and the unfavorable trading conditions requiring access to British pounds caused the American War of Independence. After the war, the Americans created the American dollar, which eventually became the most widely used currency globally. The American dollar still holds that honor.

---

3 Cammiade, A. (1967). Franklin and the War of American Independence. Routledge.

In the 19th century, banking became a respectable business. Banks made money by lending money. They paid a lower interest rate for money they received from customers but charged higher interest on loans (what a great racket!). Banks also lend out more money than they have on deposit because they assume that their customers won't all ask for their money at once.

After the global financial meltdown in 2008, economists distinguished between two kinds of money. First, banks create money inside the banking system. Second, governments make money outside the banking system. So, for example, when banks create a new customer loan, this is money made inside the banking system.

Governments create money by selling new bonds, which circulate as new private assets. This government money adds to the public debt. In the United States, the government used these bonds to buy up the banks' bad personal debts and write them off in 2008. In turn, the private sector retained its wealth inside the system with support from the government's public debt outside the system.

Despite the United States borrowing billions for its bank rescue and stimulus plan, which dramatically increased the supply of dollars, inflation and exchange rate depreciation did not happen. The world continued to trade in American dollars. Perhaps it is faith in the almighty dollar's value that keeps the dollar strong.

Today, thousands of years since the invention of money, only about two percent of the world's transactions occur in coins or paper money. Instead, most transactions are with credit cards and electronic banking. Digital technology enables new currencies like Linden dollars, Bitcoin, Ethereum, and other cryptocurrencies. However, these currencies retain the characteristics of money, such as being hard to forge, durable, portable, divisible, and limited in supply.

Digital currency never takes a physical form, unlike other electronic banking transactions. For example, right now, if you go to an automated teller machine (ATM), you could withdraw your holdings in physical dollars (or other currency, as the case may be). However, cryptocurrency always remains on a computer network and is only exchanged digitally—you cannot touch it physically since there is no tangible object. Functionally, this is no different than how we currently use payment applications like PayPal or Apple Pay.

The interesting thing about cryptocurrency is that it is currently not managed by a central authority, such as governments and central banks. However, governments and banks are researching creating digital currencies, called central bank digital currencies. Think of this central bank digital currency like Bitcoin, except that this Bitcoin's manager is the federal reserve and backed by the government. Interestingly, at least 80 percent of central banks are currently researching this technology.[4] Anyway, stay tuned. I'm sure that we have not heard the last on cryptocurrency. It may only be the beginning of a new way of doing business.

---

4 Rodeck, D., & Curry, B. (2021, April 1). Digital currency: The future of your money. Forbes Advisor.

In Control

(First published on July 2, 2020)

Life is sometimes crazy, isn't it? I mean, look at what we have gone through in just a few short months this year.

A pandemic killed the world economy and dramatically increased mental health cases.

Racism pushed its way into the limelight, temporarily quashing pandemic concerns while protesters took to the streets.

We expanded our vocabulary with new phrases and word pairings. "Physical distancing." "Social distancing." "We're in this together." "Stay safe." If you are like me, hearing these words is like hearing nails grating on a chalkboard. Despite everything, however, the earth continues to revolve around the sun 24/7.

What awaits us in the bigger picture is anyone's guess, but one thing is sure: With all the turbulence of 2020 (we did not lose the irony of hindsight in that number), we do see goodness emerging both in people and our planet.

Since working at home has become the norm for most, parents are now focusing more on their children. As a result, family time and the family unit have once again become relevant.

And pollution has decreased. The earth is breathing freely again.

As I ponder the first half of 2020, I wanted to share what I believe are essential learnings.

1. There is but one race on our planet. It is called the human race.

2. Money is power, and the powerful continue to rule the world. That said, the assimilation of wealth in the hands of a few (the one percent) is not sustainable for humanity.

3. Medical experts do not always get it right. Pandemic measures done in excess create more harm than good (for example, domestic violence is rising,[5] and suicide rates are spiking[6]).

4. Objective news reporting has given way to sensationalism. Ratings and profits are driving what should be unbiased and balanced news.

5. Social media creates stress in excess. It can usurp all energy in a single post.

---

5 Pawlitza, L. (2020, June 2). No surge in domestic violence cases during COVID-19 lockdown—That doesn't mean it's not happening. Financial Post.

6 Carey, B. (2020, May 19). Is the pandemic sparking suicide? The New York Times.

6. Fear makes people do silly things. Unfortunately, the media is an excellent incubator of fear.

7. All individuals function at different emotional levels. That is what makes us unique. Unfortunately, that is also what creates severe differences of opinion and conflict. Media helps fuel these differences.

8. Critical thinking is not something that everyone possesses equally. There is also inequality in the distribution of money. And power. See point 2 above.

9. Politics are a dirty business. Even good politicians must take a certain amount of mudslinging if they are to stay in the game.

10. Businesses are opening slowly, and grocery store food lines are starting to go by the wayside. Finally, things appear to be returning to normal.

11. Personal productivity and motivation are inextricably linked. Likewise, good mental health also impacts motivation.

12. Not all businesses will survive the economic slowdown. But not all companies will die, either.

I'm sure you can add more to this list.

When this pandemic passes – and it will – I hope that you get a chance to reflect on how the experience has changed not only your business but you, personally.

How will your post-pandemic reality look? Will it be the same as pre-pandemic, or will the scars remain long after the "all clear" from epidemiologists and governments?

Whatever your reality, know that businesses cannot operate as usual in the post-pandemic era. If you did not embed innovation and flexibility in your business previously, they must become part of your business mantra now. Companies capable of thinking through new ideas and quickly experimenting are the ones that will survive post-pandemic.

According to the World Economic Forum, the global economic slowdown will cost[7] at least $1 trillion in 2020 (not including the tragic human consequences). That should be motivation enough to start thinking about adapting your business to a new reality – regardless of whether a new way of doing business is required.

How do you start adapting your business? Look at the flaws in your organization first – this crisis amplified these flaws. Implementing new

---

7 United Nations. (2020, March 17). This is how much the coronavirus will cost eh world's economy according to the U.N. World Economic Forum.

ways of dealing with the customer is mandatory in correcting the weaknesses.

Next, identify where you need help – is it knowledge, skill, products, or something else? We can't do everything on our own – ask and get the help you need to sustain your operation.

Other evaluation areas include your data and technology (is it working for or against you?) and your workforce. Machines and computers are great (when and where needed), but no business can function effectively without a competent workforce.

In the end, when things do return to normal, know that you are in control – both of your personal and business futures.

Meetings – They Aren't Cheap

(First published on February 1, 2020)

If you spend most of your days in meetings but take for granted that it is just part of your job, you're wrong. Because meetings may be part of the job description, some sound judgment is needed to determine whether you should attend every meeting. After all, someone (the organization) needs to pay for every meeting attendee. And if your meetings are not effective or efficient, the cost is even greater.

Consider the following.

- An average meeting lasts one hour.

- An average meeting has about five participants.

- Assume that the average annual salary for each of the participants is $100,000.

- The cost in terms of salary for your meeting is $2,500. This cost does not include unknown or hidden costs such as lost opportunity costs, i.e., what you or your employees may have completed if you weren't in the meeting.

Now consider how many such meetings occur each day in your organization (multiply that to get your annual count). You get the idea of how quickly money and productivity are blown away on unnecessary meetings.

Next time you need to convene a meeting, ask yourself if the whole department needs to attend. And when you receive a meeting invitation, ask what contribution you are required to make at the meeting that you could not do outside of the meeting? You'll be pleasantly surprised at how much time you'll gain each week when you become very selective of which meetings to attend.

The Competitive Edge

(First published on February 10, 2019)

What's your competitive edge? What makes you or your business the "one" to beat?

If you're like most businesses, you probably say that you're good at what you do or that you're better than anyone else in your craft. That's all well and good, but why should clients care?

Here's the thing: Clients don't care about you or your business. They only care about themselves and what you or your company can do for them. This approach makes sense since clients want as much value as they can get, but they don't typically care where they get it.

What can you or your organization do to position yourselves to be the best? Here are four considerations:

Cost

Reducing operating costs will provide you with a competitive advantage in the marketplace. Relentlessly pursue the removal of all waste in your organization to reduce operating costs. Look at the entire cost structure of your organization for all potential cost-reduction areas. And don't forget to pursue Lean production in all you do.

Speed

Make sure you can deliver on your promises quickly and by no later than promised due dates. You can improve the speed of delivery by improving your organization's communications capabilities (think: Technology) and using the reliable and right equipment for the job. In addition, ensure you have knowledgeable workers to assist with your projects. And use just-in-time production to reduce inventories and reduce risk.

Quality

While some companies employ quality as a reaction to the marketplace, to compete on quality means that you and your organization use it to please the customer and not just a way to avoid problems. Furthermore, since quality is different for each customer, you and your organization need to understand your customers' needs, wants, and requirements to translate them into exact specifications for their desired goods and services.

Flexibility

Competing on flexibility means that your organization can adjust to market changes relating to its product mix, volume, or design. This flexibility means producing a variety of goods or services within the same facility to meet customized requests. Multi-skilled workers and excess capacity in the business can help an organization compete on flexibility.

Most organizations should start positioning themselves in the market by focusing first on quality. Then, once you perfect your product or service quality, focus on speed of delivery, cost-cutting in operations, and flexibility.

If your organization is not as competitive as you believe it should be, improving all of the above competitive advantages may be in order. As you become more competitive, you will find that you will reach a point where you will need a trade-off between being better in one or another area. This trade-off will ultimately set you apart from your competition.

The Lightness of Black Friday

(First published on November 28, 2018)

According to Kevin Roose of the Daily Intelligencer, Black Friday is a nationwide experiment in consumer irrationality, dressed up as a cheerful holiday add-on.[8]

It's hard to disagree with the assertion.

The problem with Black Friday is not so much the consumer irrationality (although that really should be a concern for society!); it is more about how suppliers both anticipate and succeed in increasing their inventory turnover by taking advantage of the irrational consumer. Is that such a bad thing?

I think it is, and here's why - first, sales days like Black Friday evoke erratic behavior and, second, these types of frantic sales force consumerism to take a back seat.

Black Friday sales are not necessarily big sales, but they are a super opportunity for suppliers to unload their burgeoning warehouses. However, this approach speaks to poor management of inventory and too much stock, at its core, implies

---

[8] Roose, K. (2012, Nov 21). Why Black Friday is a behavioral economist's nightmare. Intelligencer.

(and typically masks) significant management issues with the company.

Excess inventory may mean that a company is placing inaccurate inventory orders. When this happens, the company holds more stock than the market demands. That's why sales like Black Friday are a welcome opportunity to unload the excess, even if it is at a discounted price.

Too much inventory creates other problems for the company, as well. For instance, too much stock takes up valuable floor and shelf space. If the item does not sell quickly, other more valuable inventory does not make it to the shelf. This occurrence is a double whammy. Not only is the poorly moving stock not selling, but neither is the good inventory.

And when companies aren't able to sell their inventory, this hurts their bottom line. Black Fridays and other types of sales days provide an opportunity for the retailer to drastically cut costs to sell their inventory, even if the sale is a net loss.

A significant concern for companies is not only the space taken up by slow-moving inventory but the associated carrying costs. These costs are typically about 30 percent of the value of total inventory. So, for instance, if the television sets at your favourite store are worth $1 million, then the carrying cost to the store of that inventory is another $300,000. Carrying costs include things like rent, utilities, and labour.

And let's not forget about waste. In a worst-case scenario (and we know this happens more often than not – even in Victoria!), companies throw out their excess inventory. This dumping of "extra" products is why it is so critical for companies to ensure that their inventory turnover is high—to reduce carrying costs and waste—both of which cut into profits.

Ultimately, the question we should be asking is: "Why do we need so much stuff?" And, why do suppliers need to meet this demand?

Consumers indeed drive demand, but it should be a corporate social responsibility on all suppliers from the acquisition of raw materials to the end seller to help everyone curb excess. But who will start first? Will the consumer refuse to engage in sales like Black Friday, thereby not assisting companies in moving their inventory? Or will it be the smart supplier who decides to stop stocking whatever the consumer wants (and, therefore, risks going out of business)? It's a difficult question indeed.

For my part, I bought a new iPhone today. Who do I blame? Me, for purchasing a product that I did not need? Or the store that stocked it and enticed me with a great price?

Letting Go

(First published on June 27, 2018)

When was the last time you tried something new? How did it make you feel? If you're adventurous, you probably felt thrilled. If you're fearful, you are probably still wondering if the experience was worth the risk. So it is with organizations. Adventurous (or proactive) organizations thrive; the fearful (or reactive) survive—just barely.

Organizations (and individuals) that cannot let go of "dead ideas" are doomed to failure. Think about how many processes your organization manages every day. How many of these processes are preventing you and your staff from being maximally productive? Why aren't the processes updated? Is it because everyone is so overworked that there is no time to address the issue?

If there is no time now to address the issue, then when? Constantly relegating issues to the backburner is like clinging to the old ways, hoping they will magically reinvent themselves. These old ways are nothing more than dead ideas. And there is no place for dead ideas in productive organizations.

The sad news is that this way of thinking does not confine itself to individuals or the executive boardroom. Governments also think this way. This inability to let go of tired thinking is decaying everyone and everything.

Much has been written about change management because change is difficult to accomplish (think about changing just one of your habits—it takes at least three months of solid effort to build a new habit). But what seems to be coming through in organizations is that all employees need to be onboard for change. This participation requires changing old ways of thinking.

So how do we let go of old ways of thinking, of dead ideas? According to Matt Miller,[9] there are three steps.

1. Identify the ideas that matter.

    Since we can't boil the ocean, pick the projects or ideas that will really make a profoundly positive impact on your organization or your life. These ideas will typically be strategic—those "sacred cow" ideas that no one has dared question until now.

---

[9] For more information, check out Matt Miller's 2009 book: The Tyranny of Dead Ideas: Letting go of the Old Ways of Thinking to Unlease a New Prosperity.

2. Understand each dead idea's "story."

This understanding comes down to identifying the root cause. How did this process become so entrenched with subprocesses? Why did this process seem to make sense in the first place? By understanding the root of the idea, it's much easier to discern an action for change.

3. Reach for new ways of thinking.

Don't dismiss ideas because they seem counterintuitive. If they seem counterintuitive, this may signify how skewed our thinking has become; entrenched with only one way of doing things. Brainstorm. Look at possibilities. By reaching for new ways of thinking, we expand our minds.

In the end, we owe it to ourselves and our organizations to continuously improve and grow. By shedding old ways of doing things and inventing and implementing new concepts, we all thrive. Don't get stuck in an outdated paradigm just because it's been there all along.

Value: Defined

(First published on February 12, 2018)

Lots of people are talking about value these days – especially in light of Lean culture.

The Merriam-Webster dictionary provides eight definitions for "value." The definitions relate to market price, luminosity, and denomination. From a business perspective, value is related to market price and the customer's perception of a fair return on an exchange.

From a Lean perspective, value is anything that the customer is willing to pay for – as long as it meets these three criteria:

1. The customer cares about it.

2. The product or service must be physically transformed, or the step toward transformation must be an essential prerequisite for another step.

3. The product or service is delivered "right the first time."

"Non-Lean" organizations sometimes have a tough time determining what it is that their customers value. But determining value is not that difficult. It comes down to ensuring that the company meets the above three criteria—all the time. Look at it this way:

- An organization with efficient processes can keep its costs down. Low costs result in a greater ability to attract more customers and translate to value for the customer.

- An organization with inefficient processes incurs higher production costs. These costs get transferred to the customer. The customer does not see this as value.

- Inefficiency can be a business killer. In this aspect, Lean organizations have the edge over non-Lean organizations.

- Lean cultures enable a waste reduction in business processes that directly contribute to value for the customer. As a result, lean cultures help businesses thrive.

If your customer values your product or services, they will pay your asking price. On the other hand, if your offering does not meet your customers' criteria for value, the customer may still pay for it, but they will most certainly be shopping around next time they want the same thing.

Next time you complete a transaction with your customer, ask them to rate the value they just received from you. Their response will tell you how well you are actually doing compared to how well you think you're doing. Consider it a reality check.

Value is the key to organizational survival. If an organization consistently delivers poor value to its customers, it goes out of business. It's that simple.

Buying Time

(First published on October 14, 2017)

Time is money. According to Wikipedia, Benjamin Franklin was the first to introduce this idiom to reference time being valuable and money wasted when a person does not use time productively. Therefore, time and productivity are about using time wisely by engaging in activities that benefit you and your organization.

But did you know that pinching pennies on business expenses can hurt an organization's bottom line in terms of productive time?

Say you earn $100,000 per year. Divide this by 1,500 hours per year, and you get $67.00 per hour. Now let's use this amount to see where your organization is saving money while losing productive time.

For instance, using less expensive transportation to attend a client meeting: taking a bus or a ferry (as the case may be) rather than booking air travel may save immediate hard cash. However, the losses in the productive time counter the cash savings. Taking a ferry between Victoria and Vancouver, for example, requires at least 3.5 hours of travel time each way (that's a whopping seven hours).

By comparison, air travel uses about two hours each way (for a total of four hours). At $67.00 per hour, it costs your organization $469 to travel by ferry versus $268 for air travel. Thus, paying for air travel will cost the organization $201 more in cash, but it gains three hours of your productive time (which is also $201 in cash). However, the organizational return in value of your work during those three hours is much higher.

Another example includes the cost of taking a taxi compared to taking a shuttle bus (even when you're on vacation!), the difference in time, and the value of your time.

And what about employee brown bag lunches? Whether you're out at a restaurant or in the boardroom, you'll still be talking business, and the change of scenery away from the office will add the creative spark needed to be more productive. That should weigh more positively than the cost of the lunch.

Other areas to consider when "time is money" include the cost of meetings that start late and therefore don't accomplish all they intended. Also, webinars versus in-person workshops are one of those blurry areas where employers might think they're saving a lot of money. Depending on the topic, the webinar may make sense, but in-person workshops are the way to go if personal interaction is essential.

The bottom line is that "uber" penny pinching does not boost productivity, nor does it provide enduring value to your organization, regardless of the economic climate. Instead, penny-pinching on business expenses and employee education quashes morale and productivity and does not significantly impact your bottom line.

Thriving or Surviving?

(First published on January 4, 2017)

What is your worst-case scenario? What will you do if: (a) you cannot prevent it from happening, or (b) you cannot mitigate the outfall from its actual occurrence?

What if the worst possible thing happens during your project, in your company, in your life? What will you do if you cannot prevent something you thought you could prevent?

It's true. Sometimes even the best thought-out plans and prepared-for scenarios are beyond our control.

Many organizations create risk management strategies and hope never to use them. Some even go beyond planning and simulate risks to test their risk mitigation strategies. But imagine environmental, financial, or other disasters that are beyond your or your risk management strategy's control, and the risk blows up your project or your organization.

What happens next is the difference between surviving and thriving.

An organization that survives will patch up the outfall from the risk and continue business with a limp, hoping to get back to pre-risk operations.

An organization that thrives will look beyond the risk, reinventing itself to become a more robust, better service provider. In short, companies that thrive are lean, to begin with, and can bounce back more vital than ever

Many companies anticipate and identify challenges and opportunities in any project. That is a typical first step. However, moving beyond the first step involves change—and change is difficult. For one thing, agile companies (those that thrive) do not emotionally attach to the corporate status quo. They are not in love with their product or service. In fact, the less emotionally attached the corporation is to its products, processes, services, etc., the easier it is to change and become a thriving organization.

A thriving enterprise reinvents itself frequently. It not only looks forward five, 10, 15, or more years down the road, but it continuously adjusts its products, processes, and services to meet the approaching challenges and opportunities. Thus, a thriving organization learns to "fail forward" to thrive. The organization develops a relentless perspective around change, challenges, and solutions-focused opportunities to enable the business to thrive.

Like love and respect for a family, revisiting and remembering the past is good, but not if it stalls your future. Organizations that preemptively make the necessary hard decisions will not only sustain their future but will thrive in doing so.

Big Data to the Rescue

(First published on March 1, 2016)

How easy is it to analyze multiple datasets and decipher consumer behaviour? It turns out that even Google can get it wrong.

Google's "Flu Trends" project set out to produce accurate maps of flu outbreaks based on searches made by Google users, but the map diverged from reality as time went on. It turned out that Google's algorithms weren't accurate enough to pick up anomalies such as the 2009 H1N1 pandemic. This inability to track reduced the data's value.

In addition to bad analytics, bad data can also produce skewed or irrelevant results. The problem for businesses, in this instance, is that they will lag behind their competitors if their data or analytics are incorrect.

Consider the difference between Uber and the taxi industry. Uber's use of good data has propelled it to become a big data company (rumoured at 800% annual growth). In contrast, the taxi industry's bad analytics, or perhaps lack of attention to data, has left it floundering offline.

In addition to bad analytics, organizations have the potential of producing bad data or not collecting the right data in the first place. For instance, collecting data just for data's sake can lead to a collection of bad data that has no value in decision making.

On the other end of the spectrum, the Central Intelligence Agency (CIA) and National Security Agency (NSA) proclaimed that "we kill people based on metadata." So potentially, big data poses serious threats to citizens. And in recent news,[10] big data has been proposed to monitor social media for signs of mental illness.

Another big trend in big data is job opportunities. Unfortunately, the market is lacking data experts. For example, in 2013, Ritchie Bros. Auctioneers could not find a single student to hire for their data expert position. So instead, they hired a professor who taught business intelligence at the University of British Columbia.

While the economy expects big data-related professional services to grow at a compound annual growth of 23 percent through 2020, a related staff shortage extends from data scientists to data architects and experts in data management.

As the Internet heats up and big data gets stronger, Rossi[11] says that "the song remains the

---

[10] O'Neil, L. (2016, March 3). New project monitors social media for signs of mental illness. CBC News.

[11] Rossi, B. (2015, December 3). Top 8 trends for big data in 2016. Information Age.

same: everyone's a data analyst, and there's never been a more exciting job." And as the future nears, time will tell if Rossi is on point about the excitement around big data or if big data turns out to be a big bust. Either way, there is no ignoring the big data trends shaping our lives. Organizations that ignore the big data trends do so at their peril.

How Great Ideas Become
Game Changers

(First published on February 22, 2016)

Do you have a great idea? Is your idea the proverbial "game-changer?" How do you know? Here are four criteria that you can use to evaluate your ideas:

1. What is the benefit of your idea? What is its return on investment?

2. What is the cost of your idea? What are its risk factors?

3. Does your idea have a strategic fit with your organization? It needs to be consistent with your organization's practices.

4. How easy will it be to implement your idea? Ease of implementation is a key criterion.

If your idea passes all the above criteria, then you possibly do have a "game changer."

Other things to consider concerning innovative ideas include:

- Most innovation is incremental.

If you have 25 percent of your organization's people making a difference every day, that will amount to a considerable change over time. Patience is a virtue.

- Innovation usually surfaces on the front lines.

For instance, it's the FedEx guy who realizes you can do things better, not FedEx management.

- The size of the organization is irrelevant when it comes to innovation.

However, bureaucracy is the enemy of innovation because it only rewards conservative victories. Be bold!

- Innovation is sensitive to both new and desired customers.

For instance, I believe it was Wayne Gretzky that said, "I don't skate after the puck; I skate to where the puck is going to be."

- Innovation requires champions, but it also requires other things like focus, resources, and priorities. It's about consistency.

For instance, if you need a fiscally prudent environment, it must be fiscally conservative every day. Through consistency, the organization can change belief systems.

- Innovation requires patience.

  Sometimes results of change can take a long time to show themselves. Remember the first bullet point above, "patience is a virtue."

- When you have a "game-changer" in hand, you need to exploit it.

  Seek out new markets. Use social media. Get noticed.

Finally, to accelerate innovation, promote its likely causes (e.g., front line workers), and exploit innovation for all its worth. After all, it's innovation that makes the world move forward.

As Peter Drucker advised, the only way to get something new is to stop doing something old. But, unfortunately, some leaders are inclined to keep trying the same things repeatedly despite unsuccessful results each time. To me, that is the definition of incompetence. To others, that may be the definition of insanity.

When to Re-Design

(First published on October 10, 2015)

When products or services saturate the marketplace, it's time to re-design your offering and start over. Of course, sometimes just some "tweaking" of the existing product or service may be all that's needed to re-invent your business. But here are five considerations for bringing in fresh offerings:

1. Listen to consumer complaints about products or services already in the marketplace.

    Manufacturers did not create three-ply toilet tissue on a whim; neither was invisible "go on dry and stay dry" deodorant created on a whim. Likewise, if you're the "complainer," what is your complaint? Maybe there's a new business opportunity in your complaint that you may wish to pursue on your own!

2. Use focus groups to test existing products.

    Observe the groups when they use the products. What's missing? What can be improved? Post-It Notes filled a big gap in the marketplace exactly because of watching someone use paper and tape. Of course,

Post-It Notes were also a happy accidental finding, but that's another story!

3. Explore niche markets.

   Check out cool websites[12] for how niche businesses solve problems. Of course, you'll probably say, "why didn't I think of that?"

4. Use new technology to re-invent existing products and services.

   How could you use technology to save time for the customer? For example, build apps that enable your customer to see how your product will look in their home before purchasing. Or provide a super-easy return process that is no-hassle and risk-free – what a concept!

5. Create new market space.

   For instance, Starbucks does not just serve coffee, but it has created a new market space by emphasizing the social value of drinking coffee. Meeting and networking at Starbucks is the goal, not drinking coffee!

   Ultimately, any design or re-design of products or services needs to keep the customer in mind. If customers like your services or

---

[12] Rouse, G. (2012, March 27). Cool examples of successful niche businesses. The Solopreneur Life.

products, your company prospers. It is as simple as that.

As a supplement to this post, in today's 2021 environment, consider creating transparency across your company by providing your employees with the company's financials and metrics, excluding payroll, of course. When employees know their company's financial position, they move toward the same goals with renewed motivation.

In addition, think about rewarding your employees with bonuses in the years when the company is profitable. No employee will ever say no to a nice bonus cheque.

Critically Creative

(First published on September 1, 2015)

Is critical thinking important in solving problems? I'm sure you'd agree with me that it is. But did you know that creative thinking could probably be just as if not more important for this purpose?

When you have a problem, what do you do? The chances are that you try to think of a solution. But thinking about a solution without first defining the *true* problem is not effective. Certainly, you'll come up with many ideas, all worthy as solutions, but will implementing the ideas solve the problem? Let me give you an example.

Carol is working on a marketing brochure for her business in the hopes of generating more business. She thinks that a brochure will help, but she's stumped for ideas for the brochure, so she takes a break to generate wording.

Now here's what's wrong with this scenario. Carol will probably come up with lots of great ideas for wording for the brochure, but what problem is she trying to solve? Is it finding the correct words for a creative brochure? No. The problem is how to generate more business.

So it is with organizations. Working on solving the wrong problems decreases overall efficiency and costs the organization more time and money in the long run. If "symptoms" are showing up in your organization (e.g., lack of business), don't mistake them for problems (e.g., inadequate marketing brochures). Before jumping to solutions, stop and discover what's causing the symptoms to understand the underlying issue(s).

One way to determine problems is by using mind maps. Mind maps help you outline the problem(s). Then, by posing questions/challenges, mind maps help you to develop ideas for possible solutions. Brainstorming can also be a helpful exercise in addition to flowcharts, force field analysis, interrelationship diagrams, and tree diagrams. Or maybe you have some other creative ways of dissecting the symptoms from the problems.

However you go about it, defining the real problem first is essential to deriving the correct solution.

Before You Buy That New iGadget

(First published on April 25, 2015)

Recent promos for the latest new technology gave me pause. And it should give you pause, too.

There is no doubt that we are a society of "must-have-the-latest-new-toy," but have you thought about what happens to your old technology – those smartphones, laptops, printers, and other energy-emitting devices that you no longer wish to use? What is your old technology doing to Mother Earth?

You might say that you are responsible and recycle your old electronics. Good for you. And I bet many recycling depots do a decent job of ensuring safe recycling practices. But some old electronics may fall through the cracks.

In August 2009, CBS revealed some startling evidence (as only 60 Minutes can!) about old electronics being shipped illegally to countries like China where the dismantling of the equipment is hurting (understatement) the people and the environment. The show is available on CBS's website (search for "Electronic Wasteland").[13] After viewing

---

[13] Pelley, S. (2008, November 9). The electronic wasteland. CBS News.

the show, if the 60 Minutes investigation does not give you pause, perhaps the following might.

A report by Liam Young and Kate Davies of the Unknown Fields Division[14] traces the supply chain of the global economy in reverse. Their research brings the point home (literally).

After the 60 Minutes exposé aired, the Chinese government tried to clean up Guiyu's booming e-waste operation. However, Young and Davies indicated that the operation did not get cleaned up; it just went underground – or, more specifically, inside.

The industry moved from the street and into peoples' houses, creating a new form of mining as a domestic industry, where a circuit board bubbles away to refine the copper next to a pot of noodles in someone's kitchen.

Are we horrified at what's happening with electronic waste in China? Of course, we say that we are, but what do we really know about the rare earth mining industry or exploited cheap labour in places like China? We focus on our work in an air-conditioned condo using laptops or talking on phones that may one day end up in an electronic wasteland.

---

[14] You can check out different expose projects on Young and Davies' website called "Unknown Fields Division"

Young and Davies collected toxic mud created from recycled technology and created "lovely" toxic sludge vases. These vases are part of an exhibit at the Victoria & Albert Museum in London, opening on April 22, 2015.

Kelsey Campbell-Dollaghan summarizes the journey of the vases in a report titled: *These Vases are Actually Made from Liquefied Smartphone Byproducts.*[15] She states that the mud making up the vessels comes from a toxic lake in Inner Mongolia. Campbell-Dollaghan brought the mud to London. A ceramicist in a hazmat suit worked to turn the mud into pottery, representing the waste created by a smartphone, laptop, and car battery.

After reading Campbell-Dollaghan's report, I learned that smartphones each have about 380 grams of toxic and radioactive waste. So, think about that the next time you answer or make a call on your smartphone.

The questions before us are simple:

1. How much newer-better-luxury stuff do we need?
2. At what point will manufacturers take responsibility for killing the planet?

---

[15] Campbell-Dollaghan, K. (2015, April 22). These vases are actually made from liquefied smartphone byproducts. Gizmodo.

3. What can we do now to reverse the damage?

The answers to the questions are probably not as simple.

Off Target

(First published on January 20, 2015)

When Target came to Canada in 2011, not only were consumers surprised that the retailer opened over one hundred stores across the country, but so was the business community. To make such a "big bang" approach, you either know what you're doing or you're taking a significant risk. Unfortunately for Target, its risk did not pay off.

Target's biggest failure was not piloting its entry to Canada with one or two stores before launching full scale. Any project manager worth their trade will tell you that starting small and building up when it makes sense to do so is the best guarantee of success.

In addition to missing the mark with their full-scale roll-out across Canada, Target missed out on the basics of operations management. For one thing, their demand forecasting appears to have been a dismal failure. If they had correctly forecast, they would have learned that Canadians preferred the U.S.-type Target stores and not reincarnations of Zellers.

Target also missed out on strategic capacity planning as well as facility layout design. In addition, their inventory systems management was absent. This finding also speaks to their lack of adequate supply chain management.

When inventory is scant (as it was at Canadian Target stores), one might reasonably presume that the retailer used the same customized just-in-time fulfillment. However, this, too, appears not to have been part of Target's strategy.

A material requirements planning or enterprise resource planning software would have helped Target manage its stocks and stores. However, we can see that even if Target had such a system, it, too, failed them.

And what about quality? Quality and price are generally prominent factors for consumers. Integrating quality into every operation element allows an organization to reduce its prices while remaining profitable. Yet, quality does not appear to have been a high priority for Target.

While one can hypothesize about Target's demise in Canada, it provides little comfort to Target employees. As well, the company itself is now targeted (pardon the pun) as a losing venture: At least, in Canada.

One thing is sure, though: Target really did miss its mark!

Government Spending:
A Cause of Inefficiency

(First published on October 2014)

We often hear that government is inefficient: They spend too much, they take too much time to provide services, they do not provide quality services, they have too many checkpoints, and so on. But who or what is government? Are employees not the heart of any organization?

Contrary to popular belief, employee performance is not the problem when it comes to efficiency. There are many very diligent and efficient employees in any industry, including the government.

The root of inefficiency in government relates to money. More specifically, because governments do not spend their own money, inefficiency can be a severe problem.

To put this into perspective, think about these four possible scenarios relating to spending money:

You spend your money on yourself.

When you spend your money on yourself, you take care with your money, trying to get the best deal (best quality for least cost).

You spend your money on somebody else.

When you spend your money on somebody else, you still take care to spend the least amount of money, but you are not as concerned about the product or service quality. For example: buying gifts for someone else.

You spend somebody else's money on yourself.

When you spend somebody else's money on yourself, your primary concern is to get the best quality. Money really is no object. For example: buying yourself a gift or enjoying dinner on "somebody else's dime."

You spend somebody else's money on somebody else.

When you have somebody else's money to spend on others, concern for the quantity of spending and quality of product and service is not a high consideration. This scenario is the situation with government spending.

Now put yourself in the government's shoes. If you have an almost unlimited supply of someone else's (i.e., taxpayer) money each year, how will you spend it? Will you give your systems and processes the due care you would if you were spending your money?

Unlike private organizations that spend money on goods and services valued by the market, government spending has no information value. Organizations that spend to meet market demand will create a profit—the value that the organization generates. If it stops generating value for its customers, it stops making money.

No matter how much money the government spends or how much output it produces, it does not know its output value. This lack of understanding output value contributes to a cycle of inefficiency in spending and outputs.

When was the last time your government told you how well they spent your money?

Types of Clients

(First published on August 29, 2014)

Let's face it. There are clients, and then there are *clients*. Great clients (or customers) are ready, willing, and able to work with experts to achieve organizational efficiencies.

And then there are *clients* who fall short on anything from initial meeting to following through with an expert's recommendations – these latter clients are wasting not only the expert's time but their own, as well.

As experts in our various fields of work, we have all run into a variety of clients. Here are some of the more common types – if you're a client, maybe you see yourself in one or more of these descriptions:

Bargainers

These clients want everything you're proposing, but they can't pay for it. Or maybe they're doing the project "under the table" and don't want to ask the "real boss" to pay for it. *Solution:* If the client does not have the money for the entire project scope, downgrade the scope – phase the project into manageable chunks.

Naysayers

These clients can't believe the project will take six months to complete. Indeed, they can do it in a fraction of the time. *Solution:* Explain why the project will take as long as outlined (perhaps a timeline depicting steps is helpful here); if the client does not believe you, suggest a mix of internal and external resources to complete the project faster. Is the client still a non-believer? Walk away.

Stealth implementers

They insist that no one else from their organization needs to be involved in the project. Just do it. *Solution:* Stress (and demonstrate with examples) how involving others in the organization will significantly enhance the success of this project and change management when implementation occurs.

Self-made experts

These clients believe they can exactly do what you're proposing without you, so why are you charging them so much? Why don't you just tell them the steps you would take and leave them to do the job? *Solution:* Walk away.

Call 9-1-1

These clients think everything is an emergency. They needed your proposal "yesterday" and the work completed within the next month. However, when you give them your proposal, you don't hear from them for six weeks. *Solution:* Develop a project timetable and meet each deadline. Build "slack" time into all steps, including client input.

Weekend schweekend

This client sends you an email at all hours of the day and night. Weekends are for working. There is no such thing as work-life balance. *Solution:* Say no when appropriate. Just because the client works all hours does not mean everyone else needs to, as well!

Committee monger

This client believes that everything needs to be decided by a committee. The result? Everything gets decided by a committee, no one takes responsibility for decisions, and decisions take longer. *Solution:* Ensure that one "point" person (typically a project champion) will sign off on all deliverables.

Wordsmiths

Do you know the ones that review your work and almost re-write the entire content? *Solution:* Set a time limit for review and stress that only key content requires consideration. Provide an example. Or hand out the report ahead of time and then convene as a group to review the feedback.

In the end, it's up to the expert to determine whether they can work with the client. If the decision is to fire the client, provide them with the name of another expert – even if it is a competitor. You'll be glad you did!

Value and Billable Hours

(First published on August 14, 2014)

Why do companies and individuals still insist on billing for services "by the hour?" If you are tracking billable hours, you are not efficient. And, even worse, you are not providing the best possible service to your customers.

When companies focus on billable hours, it may be detrimental to other essential activities, like building capacity to serve customers better. However, this is a Catch-22 situation: You cannot bill for your time as you build capacity to serve your customers better. Then when you use this new capacity to serve customers, you discover that it takes less time to provide the same service. So if you are billing by the hour and are very efficient, you cannot earn as much as someone who is less efficient in providing the same service.

This efficiency vs. inefficiency is why billing based on the value of service provided makes so much more sense. Why wouldn't your customer want to pay you the same (or more) for a service that you can deliver in less time?

According to Canadian statistics, the amount of time spent at work is decreasing. This decrease is also the case in the United States.

Does this mean that "billing-by-the-hour companies" are earning less? Perhaps, but it might be that these same companies realize that it is more economical (and profitable) to bill for value rather than hours.

The secret to creating value for both parties (the company or person providing the service and the company or person receiving the service) focuses on outcomes rather than inputs. For example, how much time it takes to create a widget or develop a plan is irrelevant to the value the widget or plan provides to the customer.

In Lean Six Sigma terms, we want to go beyond just meeting our customer's needs and wants – we want to be sure our customer is delighted with the product or service they purchase from us. This customer delight is value. And it has nothing to do with money.

If customers are delighted with the service provided by your staff, they will pay your asking price to continue to receive this value. So it is irrelevant to the delighted customer that it cost you $100 to produce the widget, but they pay you $1,000 for the same widget.

In addition, fixed fees (i.e., value-based fees) have the advantage of using up less administrative time for both sides. There is no need to track hours unless the provider of the service wishes to do so. This approach improves efficiency for both sides.

In the end, no one cares about how good you are at your craft. Clients only care about how good they will be after you serve them. And that is the ultimate goal of any service or product.

Time and Money—An Organizational Focus

(First published on June 18, 2013)

Poorly run organizations waste time (and time is money). This waste inhibits the company's ability to hit markets at optimum times. Allow me to give you an example

Several years ago, I worked with a company in the wastewater treatment industry that consistently put in long hours to meet deadlines. Why all the long hours? The owners relied on one individual to make all the decisions. This approach was far from the wise use of corporate time and resources. The result was burn-out, missed deadlines, and in the end, the company went out of business.

An inaccurate assessment of the time needed to conduct a project, write a report, develop a product, etc., is critical to organizational success. If the estimate of time is over or under, wasted money is the result. And if your company is in the business of bringing products to market, the window of opportunity is open only for so long.

Another considerable time and money guzzler that takes away from strategic organizational focus is technology. If an organization is "wedded" to its technology and refuses to alter its approach, it often consumes more cash before realizing too late that it must change direction. Don't keep throwing good money into bad software under the assumption that it costs less to "update" what you already have. It usually doesn't.

A recent client was sometimes spending upwards of seven or more hours trying to print a 15-page report. If the software is causing so much wasted time, why spend time and money trying to fix a problem that no one can fix in all likelihood? Stop, scrap, and start over to save money. Unfortunately, knowing when to let go of technology is an underestimated management skill.

Mismanaged organizations consume budgets without ever hitting milestones necessary to achieve success. In the process, they produce frustrated and burned-out staff along with the possibility of business shut-down.

Don't be afraid to let go of products and processes that no longer work effectively or efficiently, regardless of the cost to replace them. In the long-term, a replacement will yield far greater productivity results.

Over the past 15 years, benchmark studies have shown that organizations reap tremendous rewards with modest or no capital investments. Some of these gains have resulted in, for example:

- Doubled outputs and profits with the same staff allocation

- Doubled productivity across all levels of the organization

- Reduced throughput time and defects by 90%

- Reduced supply chain inventory by 75%

- Reduced space and unit costs by 50%

What's your organization doing? Is it surviving or thriving? If it's not thriving, look at how your staff is using their time. You may be surprised at the potential savings through simple changes.

What Happened to Achievement?

(First published on May 14, 2013)

Several years ago, my son came home from school with a report card that mainly included B's and A's. When asked about the B's, he responded that his teacher said "B's" were good. His teacher told him that it's okay to strive for B's or even C's ("as long as you pass")—and not work so hard to get A's.

We have become a society of underachievers.

Consider these facts: workaholics have higher social status, exceptional achievers live longer, and the 14 most workaholic nations[16] in the world produce most of the world's GDP.

It's not uncommon to hear complaints about how much email and smartphones have taken over our lives. But let's get serious for a minute. Has technology taken over our lives? Or are we saying we're overworked because technology runs our lives?

When we let technology run our lives, we end up wasting time on email, cell phones, playing

---

16 Goldman, L. (2011, February 25). The 14 most workaholic countries in the world. Insider.

games on smartphones or computers, so much so that we become underachievers. Underachievers don't complain about working hard on the trivial, but a proclamation of "overwork" is made when working hard on the important.

The world's most influential people, such as Steve Jobs, J. K. Rowling, Oprah Winfrey, Barack Obama, and others, rise to the top because they worked (and continue to work) hard to accomplish the important. Their passions drive them to succeed. These people are not overworked. It is not possible to be overworked if you love what you are doing.

For those that underachieve and proclaim to be overworked, perhaps the blame rests with personal coaches, bosses, teachers, and other authority figures—those who say, "There, there, you will do better next time."

Failure does not guarantee success next time. And giving an "'atta boy" for each failure only reinforces the failure.

With continued underachievement comes a threat to our society's general level of ambition. Chamorro-Premuzic[17] observes that the younger generation is different based on geographic region. For example, in China and East Asia, he noticed

---

17 Chamorro-Premuzic, T. (2014, January 24). Are millennials as bas as we think? The Guardian.

that Gen Y is ambitious, similar to post-Second World War Americans and Canadians, who took advantage of a booming economy to set out to run the world.

Now ambition is withering. Generations don't work as hard to get what they want. They surrender and appear content with unavailability. However, in the rest of the world, when people want something, they work to get what they want. There is no surrender.

The way to become an achiever and never be overworked again is to stop working in a nine-to-five job, get a career, and embrace hard work. These are the only ways to succeed—both personally and for your organization.

The Leader's Role in Productivity

(First published on May 9, 2013)

An organization's performance directly links to its leader's effectiveness. Extraordinary leaders can make extraordinary employees out of average employees, while poor leaders can turn outstanding employees into poor performers. And it has nothing to do with the organization's systems, processes, policies, or procedures.

Their leader's behavior impacts employees. A McKinsey Global Survey published in October 2009[18] identified nine critical leadership skills. Inspiring employees ranked number one.

Inspiring employees is crucial if you want them to serve customers in the best possible way, all the time. Since they are the organization's front line to customer service, employees are its key to success. Empowered employees will perform their best to achieve their organization's goals. It is essential not to understate the leader's role in positively influencing this behavior.

To sustain inspiration and empowerment, employees need recognition and reward, including

---

[18] Barsh, J., & De Smet A. (2009, October 1). Centered leadership through the crisis: McKinsey survey results.

monetary and non-monetary rewards. For example, some employees may need a bonus to settle personal debts, while others may appreciate a more flexible working schedule. Ask your employees how they want to be rewarded and act accordingly.

While difficult to measure, strong leaders can impact the work environment by improving employee morale through a "snowball effect" of positive outcomes. It takes just one employee to hinder change, but one employee also creates positive effects. It starts with leaders.

There are five areas that every leader should consider to better influence productivity in their organizations. These areas are:

Defining goals and objectives

Employees need clarity around organizational goals and objectives and how projects fit within these goals and objectives. When employees understand the projects on which they are working, they can better identify and close gaps between the projects and the organizational goals.

Assigning ownership

For any work undertaken in the organization, there should only be one owner of the work. When one owner-employee takes responsibility for the project, there is a greater chance of project success. Conversely, if there are multiple owners or if ownership is not clear, efficiency and productivity suffer.

Managing employee expectations

This item includes ensuring employee job satisfaction and providing incentives and rewards. Job satisfaction increases if employees are empowered and receive appropriate support (e.g., training, resources, etc.) to complete their work. In addition, recognizing and rewarding employees helps increase their self-esteem and further strengthens their resolve to continue working hard on behalf of the organization.

Communicating

Communication is a two-way experience. Leaders need to be clear in their communications with employees, but they also need to listen to their employees and act on what their employees are telling them. By engaging in open communication, leaders build trust with their teams, further empowering productivity.

Innovating

Without innovation, organizations will not grow. Therefore, leaders need to embrace innovation and encourage innovation and creativity in the workplace. Same old, same old has no place in organizations that want to be successful. Creating or inventing/re-inventing new markets, products and services—this is how successful organizations thrive.

Leadership competency models provide boundless traits and behaviors that differentiate between good and great leaders; they are all useful. But when organizations desire higher productivity levels, then specific behaviors—defining goals and objectives, assigning ownership, managing employee expectations, communicating, and innovating—should be the achievement goals of every leader.

A core business goal, productivity, is under the direction of leaders. Leaders who can motivate and inspire their employees will be the leaders of successful organizations. Those who do not may soon find themselves out of work.

Clutter: If it's Organized, is it Still Clutter?

(First published on May 6, 2013)

Understanding what constitutes clutter from an organizational perspective helps staff eliminate clutter—both electronic and physical. While experts agree that there is more to clutter than just physical and electronic space, the organization's primary concern needs to be in these two areas and include the following categories:

Unused items

Unused items are a collection of "things" (hardcopy papers, knickknacks, electronic files, e-mail, etc.) that people keep for "just in case" reasons. *Solution:* If the item does not contribute to the organization's vision, mission, or values, discard it.

Disorganized items

Disorganized items are a collection of things one keeps in piles on desks, on floors, randomly placed on surfaces, or randomly organized in electronic file folders. *Solution:* Conduct a "purge party" to organize value items and develop a classification system to manage records and files.

Unfinished work

We typically see unfinished work in various to-do "piles" in individual offices. If several projects are on the go, there is a good chance that the individual will not complete on time if they are accustomed to gathering unfinished work. *Solution:* Delegate unfinished work to those who have the skills and time to complete it or outsource the project.

Congested space

When too many things accumulate in too small a space, the typical response is that more space is needed. The fact is that there is always more space than is required. *Solution:* Conduct a purge party to eliminate clutter from offices and computers.

To successfully rid clutter from your organization, convene a meeting to address the problem and relay the organization's vision, mission, and values. Using these elements as a foundation, explain how clutter opposes these elements. The key is to "eliminate" clutter so that the organization achieves improved workflow and efficiency.

Moving clutter around by "organizing" it in a different way does nothing to solve the problem. And it is a problem—the monetary cost of clutter to organizational and personal efficiency and productivity can be substantial.

In a 2012 survey by Forbes, 35% of workers said they would "be ashamed if anyone caught a glimpse of their cluttered workspace," and 40% criticized their co-workers' clutter.

In addition, the average worker spends 30 minutes per day and 150 hours per year looking for information. The cost to the organization for this alone is about $4,500 per year per worker. A study by Brother International found that clutter costs U.S. corporations $177 billion annually.

While some clutter costs may seem large (or small), other costs are not easily quantifiable. For example, what about missed meetings because of "lost" meeting notices in e-mail inboxes? Do organizations know how much business is lost each year because of their employees missing (or showing up late for) meetings with prospective customers?

Another impact of clutter seldom considered by organizations is the number of late fees or penalties for late bill payments. What effect do regular late payments have on your organization's credit rating?

Privacy of information and identity theft is another consideration for organizations with clutter. When too much paper accumulates, sometimes the easy way is to throw it out, but that creates risk for the organization. Instead, diligently and regularly shredding unneeded documents assures customers that the organization is serious about protecting their identity and confidentiality.

In addition to the monetary cost of clutter, there are non-monetary costs. These can include stress, overwhelm, procrastination, and many other personal impacts affecting organizational wellbeing. When environments are clutter-free, the mind is also free to be inspired with new ideas and new opportunities that will help move the organization to more profitability.

Technology and Social Media on a Collusion Course

(First published on April 11, 2013)

In the olden days (remember those?), technology didn't have a place at work other than a tool to get the job done faster. Today, technology in the workplace is much different than it was even a decade ago.

The email has coupled with instant messaging, texting has coupled with mobile phones, and other applications like Facebook, LinkedIn, Twitter, HootSuite, Klout, Ping, etc.— the list is almost endless—seem to be must-haves for businesses and individuals alike.

These technological aids invading the workplace no longer allow users to get their work done faster in an organization laden with "tradition." Instead, the collusion (yes, you read that correctly; I intended to say "collusion") of technology and social media in the business environment is having the opposite effect.

The complexities inside a business need an overhaul, including updating policies and procedures to include technology wherever possible. For instance, why use "approved" corporate travel agents when booking online is much faster? Get rid of your travel department (or travel roles) and allow employees to book for themselves. Allowing employees to use technology (like online travel booking) rather than relying on "tried and true" in-house processes can help speed up business.

And forget about middle management taking recommendations to upper management for decisions.

Organizations should either do away with middle management or trust middle management (and other front-line staff) to make decisions on behalf of the organization.

The hierarchical structure of the old no longer fits the technological revolution. If your organization is trying to include technology into its deep hierarchy, it's doing it wrong, and the approach is hurting its bottom line. Deep hierarchies suck both efficiency and productivity out of the organization. It's probably not an overstatement to say that deep hierarchies suck the life out of organizations.

Employees can only be productive if organizations efficiently manage the bombardment of technology. Give your employees access to all the information they need, so they (and only they) can decide what information is important to be effective in their jobs. Essentially, it's about employers loosening the "controls" on what their employees may (or may not) access.

Productivity and results matter more than the steps taken to get there. But if technology enables those steps, then productivity is also improved.

Employers that trust and value their employees will reap the results of improved efficiency and productivity and, ultimately, corporate success. Allow your employees to use a full range of technology to manage their jobs in the best way they see fit.

When this happens, your employees will also trust you and the organization's leadership. The result is a win-win relationship that enables the company's success.

Successful Solutions

(first published on January 1, 2013)

You may have heard that money isn't everything. While that may be true, organizations that are not making money soon go out of business. Whether your organization thrives or fails depends on where it focuses its energy; and how well it manages its money.

Focusing on the right stuff means spending even more time on things that the organization is doing well. It also means spending sufficient time on improving things that may be hurting the business. For example, if your customers love doing business with you, find out what they love and keep doing more of that. But if your competition is more profitable, find out what your organization can do better to beat the competition. Are your prices too low/too high? Are your product or service offerings limiting the company's growth? Is your organization adequately staffed?

One of the best ways to help your organization implement desired solutions is to research a comprehensive assessment of your current state. Then decide on what new products or services to implement.

When implementing solutions, there are four phases to consider:

Design

This phase identifies goals for the project. It is also called the planning phase. Items covered in this phase include identifying pilot areas, how long pilots will run, and project team members. Considerations for the design phase include developing contingency plans to minimize risk. This phase requires capturing information about things that work well and things that need improvement.

Pilot

The pilot phase should be a small-scale implementation that is easily reversible if it does not work as planned. Increased employee involvement is essential and desired in this phase.

Implementation

Implementation is the phase that sees a fully implemented solution. It is also an opportunity to debug and fine-tune the process. Training for all staff is mandatory during this phase.

Sustain and improve

After implementing your solution, identify key input, process, and output metrics (i.e., how will you measure success?). Then, conduct weekly and monthly reviews to ensure your solution is sustainable. Improve where necessary. Also, keep employees involved.

Most newly implemented solutions do not do well in the fourth phase (sustain) due to overconfidence in successful implementation. However, the fourth phase is critical to ensuring the long-term success of the gains.

Other pitfalls of solutions include failure to pilot the chosen solution on a small scale before full-scale implementation. "Big bang" is not always the best approach. Only a pilot study can help increase chances for success and minimize risk.

The Hidden Cost of Re-work

(First published on December 1, 2012)

One of the biggest problems in business processes is re-work. Anything that has to be re-done, re-built, re-packaged, or re-anything is a waste. If the service or product is incorrect the first time, then the individual (and the organization) experiences re-work, resulting in more time, materials, and cost to the final service or product. If you work by the hour, re-working your deliverable may look like you're getting paid a lot to produce very little. And you'd be correct.

Producing quality products or services the first time is vital to the organization and the employee. Think about the last time you had to re-work something. How did you feel? The chances are that you thought (and were) distracted and frustrated that you had to stop work on one task to handle something you thought you completed.

The simple act of stopping one task to re-work another takes not only the actual stop and start time, but distractions themselves make time loss more significant than the re-work itself. Experts estimate that 40 percent of the time, those that stop a task to do something else (like re-work), do not return to the original task.

Let's face it. We're not perfect. At some point, we all re-worked something. Mistakes are normal. However, if you spend more than 15 percent of your time on re-work, either the way you work or the overall process itself needs repair. Some examples that contribute to re-work include lack of clarity about the work, lack of process controls, poor quality of incoming materials, poor work instructions, inadequate training, projects that do not include true business outcomes, or other causes.

While re-work decreases the value of the process in most cases, there are instances where a type of re-work is desirable. For example, revisiting and reviewing previously completed work is both desirable and necessary for inspiration and creativity.

What worked well in previous projects? What could improve? If you don't review previous work, it is hard to answer those questions and prevent the same mistakes. One might argue that reviewing completed work is not re-work since it adds value to new work.

Here are five ways to decrease the amount of time you spend on re-work:

1. Maintain an effective records and information management system.

   One of the biggest problems in offices is that they can't find what they're looking for or base decisions on non-current information. If your information resources aren't current, there is a high probability that your decisions will need re-work.

2. Consolidate your paper and electronic records.

   Don't duplicate the same information across multiple media. This duplication creates confusion about what copy is the official version and can be a source of re-work.

3. Ensure that work procedures are current.

   Relying on procedures written five years ago is not good business. Procedure manuals are dynamic documents and need review annually to ensure accuracy and efficiency.

4. Involve those that do the work when writing procedures.

   They will provide you with the best insight and expertise about how you can do the work accurately and efficiently.

5. Use the latest technology where it makes sense to do so.

   If you expect efficiency and productivity from your employees, give them the tools to help them zip through their tasks. Buying the latest technology for them will improve their productivity. But don't buy high-priced tech gadgets if all they need to do is check their email. Less costly solutions may better suit these instances.

Pay attention to how much time your organization is spending on re-work.

Reducing re-work will enable work to get done faster at a reduced cost. In effect, you will experience a triple benefit - reduced re-work, reduced duration, and a reduced cost. Astute organizations would welcome these types of reductions.

Workplace Faults

(First published on November 1, 2012)

Between 70 and 90 percent of workplace errors are attributed to "human error" (also known as "operator error"). On the surface, one would presume that this means that the person doing the work makes a mistake independently, without the influence of other factors.

However, we know this is not entirely true. For example, human error can occur due to a person's inability to perform a required operation, but it can also occur when procedures or visual cues are incorrect.

When an organization experiences high incidences of product or service defects, equipment malfunctions, environmental hazards, and other similar defects, the most likely source of the defect is in the standards, procedures, instructions, workplace layout, workplace culture, staff morale, or other broader contributors.

It is rarely the sole result of the individual's performance. But when it results from the individual's performance, other factors may also play a crucial role.

If your organization experiences a large rate of defects from human error, consider the following.

Match the person to the task.

Not all people are created equal, and not all people can do the same tasks. However, each of us is very capable of doing at least one task very well. Find the innate ability in your staff and watch them and your organization glow.

The more complex, dangerous, unpleasant, or repetitive a task, the more likely human error will occur.

For these types of tasks, consider assigning more than one person. This way, more breaks can be taken so that the individual can provide complete focus to the job with less chance of errors.

Ensure that procedures are current and that staff receives training.

If not, staff will make best guesses about how to complete tasks, and this increases errors.

Fatigue can increase human error.

One needs to be at their best (i.e., sleep is a major contributor to a person's well-being) to perform their best. If staff works long hours to meet deadlines, the quality of work may suffer due to human error.

Illness, injury, stress, and other personal factors may contribute to human error.

In addition to ensuring one is well-rested, staff experiencing illness, injury, or stress need to take responsibility for their well-being to be high functioning in all aspects of their life. Human error abounds when one is not at their best.

It is human nature to want to blame a person for a failure. It is somehow easier to blame a person than for the organization to admit deficiencies in its procedures, products, services, processes, or systems. And in some instances, it may even seem less costly to outright fire a worker for their errors than look at the more significant issues. But a study by Shanders and Shaw (1988) revealed that in no case is human error the only factor.

To reduce human error and improve your organization's quality of work, consider implementing a Lean Six Sigma approach. By doing so, you will experience better speed, better flow of work, reduced defects, and reduced process variation. This improvement means better quality faster with a reduction in cost and complexity of products and services.

Braking Waste

(First published on October 1, 2012)

According to an analysis conducted by Nokia Seimens, overall industry profits could rise by 13 percent if all service providers operated at the same high level of performance as the market leaders. If your organization is not a high-level performer, it is likely due to wasted time, materials, or money. Profitable organizations are putting the brakes on waste.

There are a few things an organization can do to increase its profits. It can raise its prices for its products and services, sell more, or lower its costs. Raising the selling price in an increasingly competitive global market probably won't help unless you've already got a top-selling brand. Selling more is a possibility, but that creates a lot of labour intensity and perhaps added marketing expense.

The third option, lowering costs, is the best. This option means that the organization becomes more efficient and effective by reducing waste and saving money—directly leading to an increased bottom line.

A profitable organization is a successful organization. Its success depends on its efficiency (doing things right) and effectiveness (doing the right things). If you believe that you can sacrifice one for the other, consider the following.

- If your organization is inefficient and ineffective, the business will die quickly.

- If your organization is inefficient but effective, the business will survive.

- If your organization is efficient but ineffective, the business will die slowly.

- If your organization is efficient and effective, the business thrives.

Given the above, is your organization dying, surviving, or thriving?

Extra! Extra!

(First published on October 12, 2012)

Are you the kind of person that cleans your house before the cleaning company arrives? Do you review a binder before (or after) giving it to your colleague for review? And, heck, who doesn't want to check three times to ensure the alarm system is on/off? All of this probably happens in the real world, but it shouldn't, especially in the workplace.

If you or others in your organization spend time "perfecting" or "ensuring" that services or products are delivered efficiently, you are inefficient. Think about all the things you accomplish in a day (either at work or home).

How much more could you accomplish if you eliminated redundant steps in processing?

Or what if you stopped multiple inspections, re-work, duplication, unnecessary reports, inadequate technology, multiple different spreadsheets across the organization used to record the same information, and other extra-processing that add no value to either the customer or to the organization (or to you, for that matter)?

Many organizations get stuck with processes layered with individual preferences instead of effectiveness. These processes not only take extra time, but they cost more, too. While it is sometimes a hard thing to correct, it is not impossible.

If you're dealing with extra-processing (i.e., doing more than the customer needs or requires), here's how to get back on the efficiency track: PUT IT IN WRITING. Clear standards, policies, procedures, and specifications will help staff perform their work in the most efficient way possible. Written instructions provide detail and clarity, and where there's detail and clarity, there's efficiency.

Another way to eliminate extra processing is to spend money on improving processes and/or automating processes. In this way, you will be able to run your operations with fewer resources. For instance, think about the multiple different spreadsheets across the organization used to record the same information.

Why not invest money to consolidate the information in a central database? By doing this, you are saving time and money in the long run.

If there is a more efficient method of getting the same or better results for your customers, it is worth an initial investment for long-term gain. This type of "extra" is good value for money rather than the extra steps built into adding no value processes.

Establishing the Need for Improvement Benchmarking

(First published on October 11, 2012)

One of the key requirements of implementing a continuous improvement program is to establish a need for improvement. You may think this is quite easy since you already "know" what needs improving. But establishing a need for improving services or products may be harder than you think.

If you can't show the need for improvement clearly and meaningfully, it will be challenging to get support for making change.

One of the best ways to establish a need for improvement is to benchmark. That is, compare one entity to another to improve internal processes. There are four types of benchmarking:

1. Process benchmarking is about reviewing and comparing process best practices of other companies.

   For example, the process of issuing building permits – how are other organizations managing this process compared to your organization? Are they faster? What is their cost of operations? Are their customers satisfied with the process?

2. Performance benchmarking relates to reviewing companies that you know are doing a better job than you are overall.

   When undertaking performance benchmarking, it is generally on competitor companies.

3. Project benchmarking is about evaluating best practices on projects similar in scope to your project(s).

   You can do this with projects both internal and external to your organization. For example, do your projects generally run over schedule? Over budget? If so, why? What do others do to enable them to stay within schedule and budget? If the Empire State Building was able to be built in 1930 under budget and ahead of schedule, what's preventing your projects from being equally successful?

4. Strategic benchmarking relates to observing how other organizations compete.

   This type of benchmarking is not industry-specific, and therefore, non-competing organizations are more willing to share their best practices for similar business processes, products, or services. In addition, organizations can learn from all operating units within their organization.

Once you know what type of benchmarking you need to undertake, there are five steps to follow. They are:

1. Determine your organization's current practices in your selected problem area and identify your organization's key performance indicators. These indicators are your starting point.

2. Identify the organization(s) from which you will be obtaining benchmark data.

3. Analyze the data you've gathered, comparing your organization's current practices to the best practices you have observed in other organizations. What are their best practices in this area? In what ways are they better than your organization? Are they faster? What is the cost of the operation? Do they produce a higher quality product/service? How is their customer satisfaction rating in this area?

4. Model the best practices to fit your organization and present a business case to management for why modeling these best practices is necessary for your organization. And when approved, implement the change.

5. Repeat the process. This step is critical since continuous improvement is not a one-off implementation project. Instead, it is a plan-do-check-act cycle that never ceases.

As a management tool, benchmarking cannot be underestimated. It helps you know "how well" your competition or internal units are doing and prioritizes change.

If your organization does not include benchmarking as part of its continuous improvement mandate, your organization is likely fighting fires and focusing on the present. Instead, use benchmarking to help your organization become and remain profitable by having more time to think about improvements and focus on the future.

Leave the firefighting to the fire department.

Money, Money, Money

(First published on October 1, 2012)

"Money, money, money" are opening lyrics in a famous Abba song. The band alludes to neverending, sunny days in a rich man's world. The song is upbeat and makes the listener believe that money is the answer to everything. While that may not exactly be the case, it is hard to deny the assertion.

When the economy seems to be plummeting, it gets harder to maintain (or build) a profit, no matter if you're a big corporation, a small business owner, or an employee. Goods and services cost more, and taxes never cease, yet you need to keep moving forward on that food chain. So, what do savvy leaders do? They look at their internal processes for cost savings.

In any given process, organizations waste an average of 30 to 50 steps. Think about your accounting process as an example. How many forms, transactions, signatures, approvals, batch reviews, etc., is your company producing or processing? Of these, how many steps add value to your customer?

If you're honest with yourself, you will see that this one function alone, once improved, could save your organization thousands of dollars with only minor changes.

Re-kindle your organization's productivity by involving staff in a Kaizen event where you will be able to identify several savings throughout your organization. The event uses "bursts" of education followed by immediate application of learning. Typical results of Kaizen events can include immediate productivity gains between 10 to 20 percent.

Here are guidelines to conduct your own Kaizen event:

- Select an area for improvement that will provide a high impact/low-risk learning experience

- Obtain management buy-in and support

- Day 1 - Train the team in Lean Six Sigma

- Day 2 - Gather and analyze baseline data information, e.g., use value stream mapping, problem-solving, error proofing, waste walks, spaghetti charts, etc.

- Day 3 - Brainstorm; set goals, and develop implementation plans

- Day 4 - Implement your plan and collect data again (to compare before and after)

- Day 5 - Prepare and do a dry run of the presentation that the team will make to management (post-Kaizen event results)

Kaizen events help your organization create flow, eliminate waste, and create urgency among participants. Since a single event can improve productivity by as much as 20 percent, expanding the event to every area of your organization will also expand your productivity gains. And with improved productivity comes more money in the bottom line.

The beauty of Kaizen events is that since staff actively implement changes, the changes are sustainable. And where there is sustainability, there is profit.

Move it or Lose it

(First published on August 15, 2012)

I remember handling a multi-copy "request for service" form that contained an area for four signatures many years ago. One of the signatures was required twice, at two different steps in the form's process. This requirement meant that one manager had to see the form twice, at two different times.

Now think about this. Here's a form initiating a service, but it is being transported between different offices multiple times. You can certainly see the problem with this process, but at the time, not a single manager thought that this form or its process was flawed. Nor did they consider how this process was impacting their customer.

Even today, many people still go through their workdays completing forms or other tasks, passing on the task to the next person in the process without questioning the process itself. But the movement of information, parts, and materials around an office (or facility) can be a tremendous source of waste.

Excess email and email attachments take up storage space and take more time to search and retrieve. In addition, multiple approvals of documents take up time, files moving between offices take time, and moving boxes from one end of the office to another to free up space is also wasteful.

This unnecessary transportation usually pairs with unnecessary motion, product damage, loss of product, and more systems to track the movement.

One frequently overlooked wasted transportation fact is that people often have to make round trips, which increases delays. If you're working in an office that keeps you moving often, you may consider yourself lucky because the movement keeps you fit; but consider what this is doing to the organization's efficiency. If you're walking 100 feet to get documents or other items 20 times a day, you're walking about 170 miles (274 kilometers) a year. This distance equals about one wasted hour per day. Fit? Yes. Efficient? No. Transporting product between processes is a cost that adds no value to the product or the customer.

Determine which processes should be next to each other by mapping the product (information) flows. This mapping makes the process easier to visualize and correct.

Commit to streamlining your processes with minimal movement within and between processes. You may just save yourself and your staff one hour each day. Instead of wasteful walking around the office, why not use that time more efficiently for a workout in your favorite gym?

Time is Money

(First published on August 1, 2012, statistics updated in 2021)

The American Time Use Survey[19] reported that employed persons spent an average of 7.6 hours working on the days that they worked.

Employees worked more hours, on average, on weekdays than on weekend days—8.0 hours compared with 5.7 hours (source: 2011 American Time Use). This time is up 11 minutes from the 2010 survey. In total, the average American worker spent 56 hours per week on work and work-related activities.

---

[19] Information obtained from the American Time Use Survey. In comparison to 2010, the survey's figures for 2020 are as follows:

Time spent working per day in 2020 = 7.6 hours; in 2019, this figure was 7.7 hours.

The pandemic impacted percentage of workers. For example, percent of employed men who worked at home increased by 16 percent from 20 percent in 2019 to 36 percent in 2020. Women working at home went from 26 percent in 2019 to 49 percent in 2020.

Statistics Canada update:

Time spent working per day in 2020 = 7.5 hours; in 2019, this figure was 7.6 hours

In 2019, men worked an average 40.1 hours per week and in 2020, 39.8 hour

Women worked the same hours in 2019 and 2020 = 35 hours per week

In 2010, 82 percent of all workers worked on the average weekday, with 35 percent working on weekends and holidays. However, this total significantly exceeds 100 percent since many worked on both weekends and weekdays. In addition, the survey found that men worked significantly longer than women (an average of 8.4 versus 7.5 hours daily—compared to 8.2 and 7.4 hours in 2010), for a total of 47 minutes more per day.

This trend is similar for workers in Canada—in 2011, on average, men spent almost six hours more per week than women—39.3 compared to 33.0 hours.

However, women are more likely to work part-time and take a more active role in family care and housework, which accounts for the differences in working longer hours than men.

The survey does not answer why people worked longer hours in 2011 than previous years, but one plausible response could be that the economic slowdown has prompted those with jobs to work longer.

Another reason is that work processes are becoming increasingly inefficient, so it takes longer to do the same tasks, and it costs more.

It takes less time to implement efficient processes than it does to maintain inefficient ones. Simply put, efficient organizations have more money. If your organization is inefficient and is laboring away its money, management must take efficiency measures seriously. Take time now to streamline processes for the sake of all your workers and your money.

Profits in RIM

(First published on July 1, 2012)

Sharing information with your employees and customers is important in maintaining good relationships. And knowing where to find information when you need it is even more critical. If your organization's information resources disable effective decision-making, you need to improve your records and information management (RIM) practices.

Information has always been and continues to be necessary. Imagine doing your work or making decisions without information, and you'll see what I mean. Unfortunately, some organizations still believe that the management of records is done only by junior administrative staff. Organizations that think this way cannot be more wrong.

In organizations without records management programs, 40 percent of records are typically not active, and 35 percent are useless. This statistic means that only 25 percent of the organization's total records volume is active, providing current information.

Organizations without RIM programs generally end up storing all their records onsite. In these instances, the organizations are spending

75 percent more for records management than necessary. On top of this, employees performing ineffective searches and wasting time looking for information can cost companies up to ten percent in salary expenses.

Organization-wide RIM programs usually pay for themselves at least once annually in documented savings to the organization. However, if you and your organization are still making excuses for not implementing RIM programs, you spend 20 to 30 percent more in annual operating costs than necessary.

On top of this, you continue to expose your organization to major legal, compliance, and business risks. Why gamble with your organization's money and reputation? A sound RIM program will enable your organization to increase its efficiencies and its bottom line.

Waste Not, Want Not

(First published on June 10, 2012)

When we think of inventory, we typically think of the manufacturing industry. Still, businesses in any sector have inventory: food, retail, service, government, not-for-profit, professional associations, etc., and it's a guarantee that the business deals with inventory. Inventory is necessary for business operations, but when supply exceeds demand, problems arise, especially in the organization's bottom line.

Take forms and publications as an example. Many organizations produce both. Now think about how many forms and publications your organization has stockpiled not only in one department but perhaps in several. Excess inventory hurts not only your bottom line but your reputation, as well.

Suppose you have an office in a bank. Also, suppose that your office has stacks of loan applications piled around your office. Now imagine what this says about you to your customer. Or if you've got outdated stationery stock or computer equipment lying around your workplace, what image are you portraying to not only your customers but to your staff, as well? On top of this, the "clutter" reduces employee morale and inhibits creativity and excellent work performance.

Having precisely the right amount of inventory to meet your turnover rate is possible. Start by determining the excess inventory's root causes and then identifying solutions to eliminate the root causes. Some root causes may include long lead times, poor forecasting accuracy, quality problems, or design obsolescence. Eliminating root causes of low-turnover inventory will prevent arbitrary year-end reductions in inventory investment.

Organizations with outstanding inventory performance also excel on other dimensions such as customer service, delivery, and productivity. And if your organization is not excelling in those areas, then it is underperforming and losing money.

Managing Overnight Success

(First published on June 7, 2012)

I recently worked with a client organization that became successful, seemingly overnight. Their dilemma was about managing their instant success and continuing down a road of high efficiency and productivity.

While instant success is a dilemma that many organizations would love to experience, one thing that struck me about my client was that they recognized very early the need for effective systems for continuous improvement. This recognition alone speaks volumes about how they will continue to be successful.

But how do successful organizations remain or become more successful? In my experience, there are three areas of focus for success. They are executive engagement, communications, and project management.

Executive engagement

When an organization is successful, its executive must continue their engagement within the organization. This engagement includes: setting clear priorities that align with the organization's initiatives and programs, using facts and data to support actions at all levels of decision-making, creating accountabilities, expectations, roles, and responsibilities for the organization, and conducting and attending regular audits/reviews to assure and verify progress.

Communications

Communication is essential to ensure that both executives and staff know what is going on within the organization, especially in terms of support for the organization's mission. All staff, but especially executives, should be active communicators. There is nothing worse than working in an organization and not knowing its plans or achievements. Provide regular written communications through newsletters, Intranet postings, or other means. Develop and disseminate communication aids to management. Organizations who are in the "know" are also in the "lead."

Project management

Ensure that your projects are well documented and that they meet your organization's priorities. Establish a one-year project inventory and update it regularly. Projects must meet critical business and customer needs. If they don't, they're not worth doing. Projects should also be of appropriate scope and size such that the projects can provide your organization with significant savings and be achievable. Above all, ensure that each project has a Champion and a Project Manager and are held accountable for project results. Use project management concepts to ensure that your projects are on track.

With these three elements constantly working within the organization, success is inevitable. But there is one more thing that I'd like to mention here – creativity.

Creativity and innovation can improve your organization's performance through executive engagement, communications, and project management.

Don't be complacent with your success.

You need to work hard to ensure continuing success. Successful organizations and successful people may not always meet their goals 100 percent of the time, but they certainly strive for 100 percent in all that they do.

Stockpiled

(First published on June 1, 2012)

Would you invest your money in a financial institution that offered you a negative 25 percent interest rate? Of course, you wouldn't do that, but many organizations quickly purchase supplies that they "may need" sometime soon. This action is the same as investing your money in a negative return.

Carrying stock is expensive, usually 20 to 40 percent of the average value per year that it costs to purchase. Still, it consumes valuable floor space in the office or may require large warehouses. It also increases material handling costs, and large stocks require computer systems for tracking and control.

Inventory management has seen more emphasis in the past decade by developing various inventory control and management techniques. However, reducing stockpiles of inventory is not just about reducing the number of orders. It includes reviewing the process of inventory management, as well. Moreover, it is about developing a self-sustaining approach rather than just looking at monetary gains in the short term.

To get a better handle on your organization's inventory and manage your stockpiles, apply the Deming cycle (Plan-Do-Check-Act) to evaluate your organization's requirements. This strategy includes observation, preparation, and planning of Lean initiatives (Plan), implementation (Do), measurement and assessment of the implementation (Check), and continuous improvement of the process (Act).

Don't underestimate the cost/value of your inventory. It can be the one thing that is contributing to decreased profits.

Productivity or Greece?

(First published on May 24, 2012)

Productivity is a very complex topic, and even among experts, it isn't easy to exact a prescription to improve productivity. But, in its simplest form, productivity measures the efficiency of production.

It is the ratio of production output to what is required (inputs) to produce the outputs. In terms of economic growth, governments look at productivity as labor based on the average number of hours each employed person works and the proportion of the entire population employed.

Labor productivity drives living standards. However, just because a person is employed does not mean that they are productive.

At the macro level, investments in physical capital, human capital, and innovation drive productivity. At the micro-level, productivity depends on the individual's ability to improve their relative standard of living through their productivity.

While investment in productivity at the macro level is necessary and important, investment at the micro-level is even more critical. Can you imagine productivity without the individual?

Investing money to hire more people, improve business infrastructure, and fund more innovation won't help if the organization isn't first managing issues directly impacting its human capital, physical capital, and innovation.

Consider the following. An organization's current workforce is not producing at expected levels, so it hires more people to improve its productivity. Is this the solution? Not necessarily. To improve productivity, first, review the process to understand the contributing factors to lack of productivity. Employees are one part of the overall process, so adding more people to the process without knowing the cause of low productivity won't solve the problem.

Other factors impacting productivity may include the equipment in use (and how the organization uses the equipment), steps in the process, how steps are executed, waiting time, information management, etc.

Consider another example. British Columbia's productivity performance is consistently below the Canadian average. One issue for this is that the province is not addressing driver-specific issues of productivity performance within areas such as human capital.

One must improve the elements that contribute to improved human capital (for example) before improving productivity and performance. This improvement includes the quality of the educational system, on-the-job training, skills shortages, the capacity of workers to serve stakeholders, etc. These are all crucial determinants of success for overall economic growth.

British Columbia lacks a "culture of productivity." This proclamation is from a report from the BC Progress Board in 2008. In recent years, other jurisdictions lacking a culture of productivity saw their economies stumble.

Paying attention now to productivity details at the lowest level will ensure a vibrant and sustainable future.

All the policies in the world won't help improve overall productivity if worker productivity is lacking. Greece learned the hard way. The rest of the world can learn from Greece.

The Big Lollapalooza: Exposed

(First published on April 25, 2012)

Lollapalooza: an extraordinary or unusual thing, person, or event; an exceptional example or instance.

When was the last time you experienced a lollapalooza? Well, these days, it seems that Lean and Six Sigma are the big lollapaloozas, although Lean and Six Sigma are nothing more than common sense approaches for efficiency.

And getting work done efficiently is never an exception to how organizations are (or should be) practicing. Along with effectiveness (doing the right job), efficiency is essential to ensuring productivity.

Efficiency has a long history. It started with scientific management in 1899 with Frederick Taylor's industrial experiments. Then it moved to Edwards Deming's Total Quality Movement (TQM) and TQM's influence on the Japanese following World War II. Then we were delighted with Peter Drucker's management philosophy in the 1980s and the Concept of the Corporation, and, of course, many other influencers in between. Their goals were to enable individuals and organizations to do their best for the least possible cost and maximum gain.

Efficiency can save you and your organization time and money, and sometimes in a big way. Let me give you an example.

Client X (not his real name) had a problem with the way his organization's decentralized branches managed and delivered services to their customer. Specifically, management felt that branches were duplicating work both within and between branches. Client X gave me an example: some branches called on each other to invite 'guest staff' from one branch to speak at another branch to share vital information that the recipient branch could incorporate into their processes. Client X needed help.

The first step to solving Client X's problem was convening key staff in one room to create a value stream (flow) map of their processes. For this initial meeting, in-person attendance was mandatory.

Using sticky notes, staff wrote and illustrated each branch's process(es). From here, the staff wrote down the time required to perform each step. When staff posted all the sticky notes on the wall, it was clear that branches duplicated multiple steps that had no value in delivering customer service. In addition, for one process alone, there were six different methods for getting the job done.

Then participants had an opportunity to pinpoint areas where delays and complexities were the greatest. With just a few simple improvements, they could eliminate 20 processes out of 40, streamline another 15, and reduce waiting time for their customers by 95%. Not bad for a couple of days' work in the boardroom!

So, did Client X and their staff have a "lollapalooza" moment? Sure, they probably did. However, my take on this instance is that efficiency and effectiveness were re-invented through Lean and Six Sigma concepts to help the organization's sagging bottom line. Lean and Six Sigma are the much-needed something new, something trendy, to encourage people and organizations to stop throwing away time and money.

If you haven't jumped on the efficiency and effectiveness bandwagon, you must have money to burn.

Benefits of Streamlined Operations

(First published on April 23, 2012)

Service organizations comprise more than 80% of the GDP in the United States and about 70% in Canada. And even within non-service companies, 80% of costs to deliver a product or service still come from support functions such as finance, human resources, and purchasing.

On top of this, work that adds no value to customers typically comprises 50% of total service costs. So you can probably see where I'm going with this, but let's talk about streamlining operations first.

What does the term "streamlined operations" mean to you? Is it about standardizing? Stabilizing? Improving? Saving? Mistake proofing? It means all of those things and more. When a client asks for assistance with streamlining operations, this implies a loss of efficiency and effectiveness in those operations, and a noticeable depleted bottom line is the client's call to action.

How does one streamline operations? The best way I know how to do this is by applying Lean concepts. Lean is about creating an environment where one uses the right resources and work to deliver a product or service to a customer.

To employ Lean concepts, start by first defining your value stream. This step includes identifying all the actions necessary to bring a product or service from concept to launch (the development value stream) and from order to delivery (the operational value stream). Then break the value stream into its parts to determine where resources and work add value in the customer's eyes.

If the work is not adding value to the end product or service to the customer, it is non-value-adding work and should be either eliminated or streamlined. In short, using Lean concepts will help you eliminate waste from your organization—wasted time, costs, and work.

One can get marked improvements by streamlining operations in almost any area, but here are the top five areas where applying Lean concepts will give you more time to do creative work and impact your organization most. You'll notice that these areas are typically an "internal" function in the organization and do not add value to the customer. Still, they are necessary, and containing waste in these areas is key to a successful organization.

Accounting

Look at all accounting functions, such as invoicing, collections, paying vendors, budgeting, reporting, auditing, payroll, and other activities. The biggest waste in accounting may be in the reporting of financial and performance measures. What happens here is that in generating reports, a lot of 'investigative' non-value-added activity may occur to read reports. The solution is to identify and address the root causes of the system issues so that the accounting system and its related processes generate accurate reports at all times. In addition, ensure that reports are easy to understand for everyone in your organization. In other words, standardize and streamline the accounting process to eliminate wasted time and effort.

Purchasing

Having only "one" way to purchase items is not always efficient. It depends on what you're purchasing. Your organization should have multiple ways to purchase goods and services. There is no need always to issue a purchase requisition or a purchase order. In addition, to truly achieve Lean operations in purchasing, it is important to establish a good relationship with your vendors. In other words, you need to provide a "complete" solution in the purchasing function, not just piecemeal purchases.

Human Resources

If your HR department is heavily involved with payroll, benefits, and compliance reporting activities, then your HR department is wasting time. HR's real work is developing the organization's human assets. The way to get HR back on track is to standardize the "hire-to-retire" value stream. Look at all the areas where waste can be eliminated and implement strategies that provide a continuous improvement culture.

Sales and Marketing

One can improve this functional area in an organization by eliminating waste in processing sales and marketing activities. The first step is to identify all the functions performed and then produce a standard template that would work in most sales and marketing situations. The keyword here is "standard." Each sales call and each marketing project consists of similar steps. Find similar steps and eliminate those that do not add value to the customer.

Customer Service

Last but not least, organizations should look at how they are managing the services they provide to their customers. Every organization, from the government to for-profit, has customers. What do customers complain about the most? Identifying most complaints would be a good starting point for identifying root causes and implementing solutions to improve customer service. Considerations include telephone answering and waiting time, quality of products or services, pricing structure (how complicated does your pricing have to be? really?)

When you've got your key areas for improvement, it's time to involve your organization. Start with developing a business case (what is it that you are trying to improve? why? What resources do you need to complete the project?). Then get senior-level buy-in. Remember that planning and managing a streamlining of operations cannot be done in a vacuum. Before starting your improvement project, ensure that you have a sufficient understanding of Lean to give you a good result. And, finally, as you work on your transformational change, ensure that you eliminate variation during the project. Do this by focusing on the problem-solving methodology of DMAIC – Define-Measure-Analyze-Improve-Control. A project charter is very helpful in this regard.

And, finally, go: Get Lean to streamline operations.

Remove Complexity to be Productive

(First published on March 18, 2012)

There are many roads to productivity, but eliminating complexity from personal and business processes is the best way to become more productive. And the way to eliminate complexity is to identify areas in your personal and/or business processes that are costing the most and/or are creating the most customer dissatisfaction in the shortest period.

Let me give you an example relating to a business process that is also impacting the personal process.

I recently worked with a client to assist him with developing better personal practices to enable him to be more productive. The biggest problem he was experiencing was not getting his work done on time. His employer felt that he was taking too long to produce a finished product. The client's long time to complete tasks was costing the organization more than necessary. And, as a result of his taking too long to finish tasks, his customers (bosses and co-workers) were becoming increasingly dissatisfied with his performance.

It would be easy to say that my client should use better time management skills and focus on performing these critical tasks to solve the problem. But it's not so clear-cut.

You see, upon analysis, I discovered that my client was indeed using good time management skills and working diligently at essential tasks, but the tasks themselves were suspect. In one instance, the task required several repetitive steps, including review and feedback from others. This back-and-forth prevented my client from completing what otherwise could have been a simple task.

For example, implemented years ago, a simple spreadsheet task steadily grew in complexity with new rules, and new decision-makers added along the way. You guessed it. With each new rule and decision point, complexity increased, and the amount of work went up. This complexity undermined my client's productivity while increasing the costs of delivering the completed task.

In this instance, instead of adding new and more rules to an existing process, the entire process should have been re-evaluated and simplified. This review would have saved time and money as well as customer (and client) angst.

You can see from this example that helping clients become more productive is not necessarily about the clients' work habits. Instead, it could relate to organizational systems and processes that have become complex over time. To remedy the situation, I suggest conducting a diagnosis to identify the causes of the symptoms (i.e., the "problems"). Then develop an action plan and implement the action items to remove complexity.

In any organization, a modest estimate is that 40 to 60 percent of activities and costs associated with services and processes do not add value to either the services or processes and do very little to satisfy the customer. By eliminating complexity, an organization can realize large productivity improvements in just a few short months.

Putting People Back into the Quality Process

(First published on February 14, 2012)

When we focus on business improvement, the easy part is fixing holes in systems and processes to gain quality and efficiency. But the key to making those fixes stick is the people. Enter positive psychology.

Positive psychology is a psychological theory that looks at the positive side of human behavior. Where psychopathology categorizes undesirable behavior, positive psychology builds on character strengths to help optimize organizational productivity.

Positive psychology is exceptionally well suited for use within culturally diverse workforces. Here's how it works in an organizational setting.

Goals

When you identify a problem, instead of blaming workers for poor performance, invite the workers to embrace the opportunity to create a new set of objectives and goals to solve the problem. In doing so, the workers improve their skills. For example, instead of pointing out that the workers' "inefficiencies and lack of productivity are inhibiting workflow," the leader says, "Let's make records management a priority and skill for improvement."

Feedback

With the problem identified, invite the worker to participate in problem-solving. The leader needs to provide specific and immediate feedback about the problem. Following our example above—inefficiencies in filing methodology cost the organization $1 million in lost productivity annually—offers a measurable and definable goal for workers using positive psychology. Providing a measure in these terms ensures that workers *really* hear the message (criticism for poor work, on the other hand, may breed hostility and more inefficiencies).

Challenge

Now that the workers understand why it is important to fix the problem (e.g., loss of one million dollars due to inefficiencies), challenge the workers to discover the root cause of the problem. For this step, leaders need to match the level of challenge to the strengths and talents of the workers invited to identify the root cause. If the challenge outmatches the workers' skills, a heightened level of anxiety can occur, counterproductive to the task at hand.

Coaching

Invite the workers to brainstorm and pilot a solution to the problem after identifying the root cause. The leader does this through coaching and mentoring the workers. Coaching and mentoring are goal-oriented and collaborative processes that encourage building on strengths to implement solutions. Building on strengths can help enhance performance. In our workflow inefficiencies example, the brainstorm solutions should focus on the workers' primary character strengths to increase their self-esteem and participation in solution implementation.

Rewards

To ensure that the solutions devised are consistently and reliably implemented, rewards are essential. Rewards should include rituals that the workers develop to help them reduce their anxiety over the new performance levels. For example, teaching the workers to use enthused and compelling self-statements ensures continuing good performance. So instead of negative thinking such as "I can't do this," the workers' self-talk includes: "What a great opportunity for me, I can expand my new learning to other areas; there's a promotion in my future."

Using positive psychology to include workers in solving organizational problems can help leaders solve vital productivity issues, improve the organization's existing skills, and ultimately improve the organization's bottom line over time.

In addition, leaders will realize a happier workforce as a result. And who doesn't want a happy work environment?

Waiting Away Your Time

(First published on January 1, 2012)

When was the last time you had to wait for something or someone? Do you remember how long you waited? If you waited for more than five minutes, you probably felt frustrated. If you waited for more than ten minutes, you might even have started getting angry about the wait. And what about those instances when you waited for hours for a service technician to show up?

While many of us have waited for products or services at least once in our lives, you may be surprised to know that there is a considerable cost in waiting. A *Cost of Waiting* study in 2011 revealed that waiting cost Americans $38 billion. This amount is the equivalent of two full workdays for every U.S. employee.

Now you might say that one can "fill in" the waiting time with other work. Still, if you have a scheduled time for a product or service, there's a good chance that you aren't going to show up on time expecting to wait for more than a couple of minutes (and even that is excessive since a zero wait time is the only acceptable number). There's little hope of recovering the lost time with any productive work when the waiting drags on.

What causes excessive wait times (those longer than ten minutes)? The answer is inefficient or ineffective systems and processes. Customers waiting in line at a bank are not waiting because the teller is slow; they wait because the process is inefficient. Files or documents waiting in a cue for a signature are not waiting because the signing authority isn't willing to sign; the waiting time is due to the inadequacies in the process or system. Is your IT system down? It's likely not due to staff; it's the process. You get the idea.

On average, 30 to 50 steps of any given process are wasteful. This waste results in any number of inefficiencies, not the least of which is waiting time. Fixing processes will result in fewer waits as well as overall improved efficiency and effectiveness. So next time you wait for an overdue report, the cable guy, attendees for a meeting, or your physician, consider this: I submit that those keeping you waiting are also disrespecting your time.

Of course, everyone may sometimes be late for an appointment or with a deliverable. However, if your scheduled person or deliverable is running late, it is courteous to those waiting to let them know how long it will be and apologize for the wait. Regardless of the cause, mutual respect for everyone's time goes a long way to keeping everyone happy during the wasted time.

More Money

(First published on January 7, 2012)

In 1972, repeated in 2004, a study showed that the percentage of very happy Americans stayed virtually unchanged at about 31 percent. This finding is even though the average income increase was about 50 percent. Other countries replicated the study's findings. But doesn't money make us happy?

It turns out that when we get more money, we are happier with more money, but only for a short while. Once we adapt to 'more money,' our happiness level drops to previous levels because now we need to acquire even more to get back to the 'high' level of happiness that we had when we got more money. To sustain our happiness then, we need to keep making more money.

But what about individuals who already have more money than they could spend in several lifetimes?

Last week, I listened to a news reporter ask Jimmy Pattison, one of the world's richest people, if he ever takes a vacation. Pattison responded that every day is a vacation for him. So, the question here is, why would one of the world's richest people continue to work so hard? Why not retire?

It turns out that those who succeed at what they do tend to keep doing more of the work that makes them successful. Their drive to succeed keeps them at their jobs, but their creativity drives them to keep raising the bar.

Their success drives them, not the money. The more one is successful, the greater the need to continue that success by sustaining an acquired happiness level. Money is just a nice side effect of success.

That is why successful people and organizations continue to be even more successful. They work hard to create success for themselves and, as a result, to increase their profits. Therefore, I would say that there is a strong possibility that the most successful and profitable organizations in the world also have the happiest employees. The common denominator? Money. So does money make one happy? Yes.

Happiness at Work and Play

(First published on December 31, 2011)

In the upcoming issue of *Extreme Profits*,[20] I write about how happy employees can help a company be successful. The flip side, of course, is how unhappy employees can drive customers away and create increased costs to the company in terms of employee turnover and hiring expenses.

While research has linked happiness to our genetic makeup, the "nature-nurture" theory certainly has a role here as well.

Our culture and upbringing bear some responsibility for our happiness, as does our socio-economic status. Still, if work continues to be a constant source of stress for you, you're not scoring points with either yourself or your employer.

Leger Marketing surveyed 58 countries in 2011, ranking their happiness based on per capita income and hope about the nation's economy.

The *Happiness Barometer for 2011* identifies Fiji as the happiest country overall. Canada

---

[20] I published this newsletter under my former company, MNC Consulting Group. An archive of the Extreme Profits newsletters are available on my website at marycolak.com.

comes in as #23, and Afghanistan fares better than the United States. Overall findings show that 53% of the world is happy compared with 13% who say they are unhappy.

So as this year comes to a close, it's an excellent opportunity for all of us to take stock of our happiness index in our work and personal lives. If you're unhappy, you need to get happy.

Make next year your year to improve your happiness.

Simplicity is Key

(First published on November 16, 2011)

Creative accounting. Insider trading. Financial fraud. Ever wonder why (or how) such corporate problems have become a part of our culture? I think it's because corporations have lost sight of the importance of maintaining an efficient workplace.

The bigger an organization gets, the bigger and more complicated its systems (and technology), the faster (or maybe slower) their service/product output, all in the name of providing more, faster, bigger to the client. But more, faster, and bigger promises, products, and services do not always result in better.

Our corporate cultures have become entrenched with the need to keep up with the competition, but they have lost their innocence and simplicity in doing so. When the focus is only on more, faster and bigger to hurry up and make money, the organization's efficiency and productivity can suffer. If efficiency and productivity suffer, so do profits.

An organization can keep up or beat the competition by first focusing on the efficiency of its operations. Efficiency enables an organization to be more productive, enabling transparency and accountability to its clients, employees, and itself.

The efficiency and transparency equate to trust. When clients trust an organization, profits are bound to go up. It's really about getting down to basics – the simplicity of how we do our work.

The 97 Percent Solution

(First published on November 2, 2011)

Edwards Deming, the father of the "quality movement," said that 97 percent of what happens to organizations is predictable and caused by the "system," not the person. Therefore, it is reasonable to presume that an organization should plan for and manage 97 percent of its operations. This planning and management include waste in overproduction, delays, unnecessary transportation, too much inventory, defective products, defective design, complicated processes, outdated equipment, and poorly trained staff.

How much of your organization's time, money, people, systems, processes, and technology adds value to your organization's product(s) or service(s)? If your answer is less than 100 percent in any area, your organization is not running an efficient operation, nor is it at its maximum profitability. By eliminating activities or resources that do not add value to the bottom line, an organization can achieve measurable, immediate, and sustainable results.

To help your organization become more efficient and help grow business quickly and cost-effectively, eliminate waste using the following steps.

Analyze your current situation.

Set the standards that your organization needs to attain by measuring its performance and comparing it to similar companies and industry best practices.

Streamline and optimize business processes.

Use diagrams and flowcharts to visualize problem areas. Removing business barriers such as silos allows immediate improvements in information sharing and decision-making across the organization.

Modernize existing assets.

Technology changes rapidly, and your organization needs to keep up if it is to remain competitive. Determine the overall effectiveness of your equipment and reduce its changeover time and downtime to remain efficient.

De-Clutter.

An organized, clean, and well-maintained workplace can help reduce and eliminate product and service delays. A visually well-organized workplace also packs a tremendous positive psychological boost for a happier workforce. (If your workforce isn't happy, it's a guarantee that your customers are also not happy!).

In addition to the above, consider that you need to identify the problem before attempting a solution. Consider what is not working first and start there with improvements.

And here's an interesting thought: No business can operate in a vacuum. One of the best things you can do for your business is create a community of practice where opportunities can open up naturally when sharing and comparing business ideas. Fostering community development could be as simple as creating public forums for discussion, creating new concepts, and providing invaluable feedback. Communities are a win-win for your customers and your business.

About the Author

Mary Čolak is the author of several newsletters and blogs on business, contentious issues, and life. *Considerations in Making Money* is her first book in the *Beyond Success* series.

For over 30 years, Mary used her unique ability to turn chaos into order for organizations and individuals alike. She helps clients identify necessary improvements in organizational and personal work methods and systems. As a result of her involvement, clients experience marked improvements in efficiency, productivity, and a reduction in their stress. In addition to working with organizations to improve business processes, Mary also coaches individuals to help them manage and overcome obstacles in their job performance. In addition, Mary taught operations management for several years as a university instructor in the Bachelor of Business Administration program.

Mary is a lifelong learner. She has a Master of Arts degree in professional communication, a Bachelor of Arts degree in psychology (major) and English (minor), and an Associate of Arts diploma in public administration. In addition, she has a master's certificate in Lean Six Sigma and was certified as a management consultant in 2004. Her awards and recognitions include the Outstanding Graduate award from the Institute of Public Administrators of Canada and an honour roll certificate from the Canadian Association of Management Consultants for placing first in British Columbia on the comprehensive national management consulting case study examination.

Mary was born in Croatia and emigrated to Canada with her parents at a very young age. Today, she loves spending summers in her native Croatia but is happy to call Canada her home, where she lives, and enjoys life with her husband, children, and grandchildren.

CPSIA information can be obtained
at www.ICGtesting.com
Printed in the USA
LVHW040157190122
708614LV00006B/200